Endorsements

Archbishop Julian Porteous is well known in Australia as a great promotor of evangelisation within the Catholic Tradition. His most recent contribution is a helpful handbook on this vital topic: "Becoming Missionary Disciples". It expands upon three panoramic topics – "the heart, head and hands" of missionary discipleship. It includes helpful questions that the reader or groups can use for further personal reflections. Archbishop Porteous reflects upon key scriptural texts on missionary discipleship. This is complemented by showcasing Australians and their personal testimonies of encountering Jesus. Then there is the journey to deeper discipleship within the Catholic Church. Locating the particular mission the Holy Spirit offers all is explained. Archbishop Porteous has a humble and conversational tone throughout the foundational subjects considered. His topics not only relate to evangelisation but also evangelise in the reading. This book is ideal for both personal and group use.
Archbishop Christopher Prowse
Chair, Australian Catholic Bishops Conference Commission for Evangelisation, Laity and Ministry.

Archbishop Porteous has long been a leader among the world's bishops in understanding and communicating the importance of evangelization. In his new book he very clearly communicates the content and motivation of evangelization and also provides very helpful spiritual and practical guidance about how to actually go about it! This is a very helpful book for anyone interested in our Church's call to participate in the mission of Jesus – and we all should be interested!
Ralph Martin S.T.D.
Director of Graduate Theology Programs in the New Evangelization, Sacred Heart Major Seminary
Archdiocese of Detroit

This new book from Archbishop Porteous offers a helpful, simple explanation of what it means to be an intentional missionary disciple. I recommend it to any Catholic who wants to deepen in personal conversion, and grow in the knowledge and techniques of bringing the good news of Jesus to our contemporaries.

Fr Ken Barker MGL
Founder, Missionaries of God's Love

Archbishop Julian on page 3 of his new book, "Becoming a Missionary Disciple" quotes Pope Paul the VI from his book Evangelli Nuntiandi - "The Church exists in order to Evangelise." I spontaneously said out aloud— "How?" The author then sets out methodically and practically a How to become a Missionary Disciple, (Evangelist). In an age where there is a How to book for absolutely everything, this little book or should I say manual is refreshingly practical and immanently valuable. Even to setting the chapters out in modules and including, a comprehensive how to prepare your testimony. Thankyou + Julian you have done a great service for the Church.

Robert Falzon
Co-founder, MenAlive

Archbishop Julian Porteous has packaged here a fresh, simple and yet powerful handbook for becoming missionary disciples of Jesus. Faithful to the content of the Tradition yet at the same time applying creativity for, sensitivity to, and penetrating insight into the contemporary cultural landscape, he brings Scripture alive and shares personal stories in what is a spiritual manual, a "practical how-to-evangelise" and a rich source of sayings from the most recent popes all rolled into one. I know I'll be buying many copies to share with friends, young people, priests and anyone interested in how to be a Spirit-filled Catholic!

Steve Lawrence

Founder and CEO, Altum Leadership Group

Leader Emmanuel Catholic Community, Melbourne

Copyright © 2023, Archbishop Julian Porteous

ALL RIGHTS RESERVED. This book contains material protected under International and Federal Copyright Laws and Treaties. Any unauthorised reprint or use of this material is prohibited. No part of this book may be reproduced or transmitted in any form or by any means, electronic or mechanical, including photocopying, recording, or by any information storage and retrieval system without express written permission from the publisher.

CONNOR COURT PUBLISHING PTY LTD
PO Box 7257
Redland Bay QLD 4165
sales@connorcourt.com
www.connorcourt.com

ISBN: 9781922815460

Cover design by Maria Giordano

Christ Washing the Disciples' Feet, c. 1520/1525,

Garofalo Ferrarese, 1481 - 1559, wikipedia commons

Printed in Australia

Every Christian is a missionary to the extent that he or she has encountered the love of God in Christ Jesus: we no longer say that we are "disciples" and "missionaries", but rather that we are always "missionary disciples."
Pope Francis, *Evangelii Gaudium*, 120

Contents

Introduction — 9

Module One – Heart: Encountering the Lord

1. The God who calls — 15
2. Encounter with Jesus — 23
3. The experience of healing — 31
4. Bringing about conversion — 39
5. Encountering the glory of the Lord — 49

Module Two – Head: Our Identity as Christians

6. The Four Truths — 59
7. Christ saves you — 67
8. Jesus is alive — 75
9. Empowered by the Spirit — 85
10. Being a disciple — 95

Module Three – Hands: Witnessing to Jesus

11. Becoming missionary disciples — 105
12. Witnessing to our faith — 117
13. How to give your testimony — 127
14. Praying with a person — 135
15. We have a treasure — 143

About the Author — 149

Introduction

Proclaiming Jesus Christ to the world has always been the essential mission of the Church. In every age the Church has had to discover afresh the ways in which this message can be most effectively proclaimed. The history of the Church reveals the extraordinary zeal of missionaries, intent on offering to others what they have known – that in Jesus Christ human life and eternal salvation find their sole purpose and realisation.

From the time of the apostolic witness, and the great missionary endeavours that led to the Christianisation of Europe, the Church entered new eras of missionary outreach into the Americas, the Far East and Africa. That the Church can truly claim to be Catholic is in that it is present in all cultures and in all parts of the earth. This is a witness to the unrelenting missionary focus which, while it may have ebbed and flowed over history, continues to be at the heart of its self-understanding.

Pope Paul VI, in his watershed document of 1975, *Evangelii Nuntiandi*, (On Proclaiming the Gospel) succinctly summarises the mission of the Church in these simple words of profound significance (EN 14),

The Church exists in order to evangelise

However, every new age must consider how this missionary mandate given by the Lord to the Apostles at the Ascension can be realised. We, here in Australia, for instance, need to consider how we can be part of the fulfilment of this task. When I say "we" I mean each baptised member of the Church. It is not just a task left to the bishop or the priests to fulfil, it is the responsibility of each member of the Church.

Each new era and, indeed, each culture, needs its own unique missionary endeavour. As Pope St Paul VI rightly pointed out, while the content of the message is unchanging, the ways and means of its proclamation will need to be adapted to the circumstances of the time and place (EN 40).

> This question of "how to evangelise" is permanently relevant, because the methods of evangelising vary according to the different circumstances of time, place and culture, and because they thereby present a certain challenge to our capacity for discovery and adaptation. On us particularly, the pastors of the Church, rests the responsibility for reshaping with boldness and wisdom, but in complete fidelity to the content of evangelisation, the means that are most suitable and effective for communicating the Gospel message to the men and women of our times.

Evangelium Project

This short book puts in written form a series of presentations given in 2022 to Catholics across Tasmania. The "Evangelium Project" was a series of three modules of five sessions given at the Cathedral Centre in Hobart and live-streamed to 23 hubs across Tasmania. Some 250 people were engaged in the program. The purpose of the project was to assist ordinary Catholics in responding to the call of Pope Francis to become "missionary disciples".

The series was broken into three separate modules titled "heart", "head" and "hands". We firstly explored the conversion experience which results from an encounter with Jesus of Nazareth. Then we explored our identity as believers. Finally, we explored some simple ways in which the average Catholic can become active as a missionary disciple.

The series was presented as a spiritual journey rather than a series of informational talks. Thus, each session began with a period of prayer including the singing of hymns. At the end of each session a question for personal reflection was presented. Those participating were encouraged to reflect on the question and then share in a small group. I would recommend that this book be used as a spiritual journey, and so encourage prayer and reflection to accompany its use.

May this handbook on being a missionary disciple inspire many to be active witnesses to Jesus Christ in a world that has lost sight of God and so needs to encounter life and salvation which is offered through Jesus Christ.

Module One

Heart: Encountering the Lord

1

The God who calls

Visiting schools as a bishop and inviting students to ask me any question they wish inevitably leads to the question: "Why did you become a priest?" Indeed, this question has emerged in many, many times in all sorts of situations. Recently I was in a restaurant at a meal with some visitors to Tasmania. I was sitting next to a young man and in the middle of the conversation he turned to me with great earnestness and asked me to tell him the story of my vocation.

That this question is posed to me – and I am sure it is the experience of all priests and consecrated people – is not surprising. A calling to become a priest is quite counter-cultural. It is often a mystery as to why someone would be drawn to embrace priestly life with its demand of celibacy, its call to total service to the mission of the Church, and to a life which is devoted to matters of the spiritual.

In the world of today with its loss of a sense of God and of the centrality of the spiritual life, it seems a vocation to the priesthood or consecrated life is a waste of one's life.

Yet to one who is a priest or a consecrated religious it is a singular source of meaning and purpose. It fosters an inner joy and contentment. Many who live their vocation would say that it is exactly who they are and who they were always meant to be.

So, many, many times I have shared my own account of my vocation to be a priest.

My vocation story

Growing up in the 1950s I experienced the normal Catholic upbringing of the times. Both Dad and Mum were Catholics. We attended weekly Sunday Mass. I went to Catholic schools. Our family was typical of Catholic families.

During the years of my primary education we were encouraged to "make a visit" to the school chapel each day as we arrived at school. I did this as a matter of normal routine.

On one of those mornings as I knelt to say my usual one-minute prayer, kneeling at the altar rails, I heard the words in my mind: "one day you will be a priest". It was completely unexpected as I had not been thinking about the priesthood. However, from that day on the idea stayed with me throughout my remaining schooling years. Upon completing high school, I entered the seminary as a student for the Archdiocese of Sydney.

Indeed, during the next seven years of seminary formation I

felt quite comfortable with the idea that I would like to be a priest and set myself to be a good priest.

It was when I was ordained that it came to me with great clarity that I was a priest not because I wanted to be a priest but because it was God who wanted me to become a priest. I spoke of this in my first homily.

I realised that my calling to be a priest was not my idea. I was simply responding to what was God's call on my life. This understanding of my vocation has remained as the bedrock of my life. I realised also that the call to be a priest was not an imposition by God but it has in fact enhanced the purpose and value of my life. As in the story of the Wedding Feast of Cana, water was being turned into wine.

I carry with myself today this simple but profound truth - that God has called me. It has also led me to the conviction that God calls others, indeed each one of us can discover the call of God upon their life.

The evidence of Sacred Scripture

That God calls people to particular vocations is seen throughout the Sacred Scriptures, both the Old and the New Testament. Let us consider some examples from the Old Testament.

In Genesis 12:1 we are given the account of the call of Abram.

> Go from your own country and your kindred and your father's

house to a land that I will show you.

Abram was about seventy years old and, one would assume, content with his life as it was, but God called him to move to another land. Abram had no idea where he was going, what he would encounter along the way but this was the call he received. God told him that he has a purpose and that he would bless him and his posterity. In Genesis 12:4 we are told simply that "Abram went".

Another example of the call of God is the story of Moses. His call came when he saw a strange phenomenon in the desert, a burning bush which was not being consumed by the fire. It is told in the book of Exodus (3:4).

> When the Lord saw that he had gone over to look, God called to him from within the bush, "Moses! Moses!". And Moses said, "Here I am."

Moses is called personally, by name. He is told of his mission in these words (Ex 4:7):

> The Lord said, "I have indeed seen the misery of my people in Egypt. I have heard them crying out because of their slave drivers, and I am concerned about their suffering".

From that moment on, Moses devoted his life to the task God had assigned him. He was to face many challenges in the process. Through it all he was faithful. He had no doubt as to what God asked him to do. Moses took it on and stayed faithfully in tune with God even though, at times, it was very challenging. Moses was called and entrusted with a mission. A call from God will include a mission of some kind, and usually it is lifelong.

In chapter six of the Book of the Prophet Isaiah, who lived some eight centuries before Christ, Isaiah had a mystical experience while praying in the temple. He saw the angels in adoration worshipping before the throne of God.

> In the year that King Uzziah died, I saw the Lord, high and exalted, seated on a throne; and the train of his robe filled the temple. Above him were seraphim, each with six wings: With two wings they covered their faces, with two they covered their feet, and with two they were flying. And they were calling to one another:
> "Holy, holy, holy is the Lord Almighty;
>   the whole earth is full of his glory."
> At the sound of their voices the doorposts and thresholds shook and the temple was filled with smoke.

An extraordinary experience. Isaiah felt completely overcome by it. He was overwhelmed and immediately conscious of his unworthiness,

> "Woe to me!" I cried. "I am ruined! For I am a man of unclean lips, and I live among a people of unclean lips, and my eyes have seen the King, the Lord Almighty."

How can we not sense our own sinfulness as we come into the contact of God's holiness? Due to this profound experience of glory of God, Isaiah was prepared to give himself totally to whatever God asked of him.

> Then I heard the voice of the Lord saying, "Whom shall I send? And who will go for us?". And I said, "Here am I. Send me!"

The Book of Isaiah is one of the most extraordinary books in the Bible. Firstly, it talks about the plans and purposes of God which reveal the majesty and glory of God as being in command of human history. It also reveals to us the story of a suffering servant, one who prefigures Jesus who will suffer and die for us on the cross.

The life of Isaiah is now totally consumed with being a prophet, a mouthpiece for God.

As a final example, we read in the opening part of the Book of Jeremiah, the prophet, (1:5) these intriguing words:

> Before I formed you in the womb, I knew you....

God had marked out his plan for Jeremiah right from the beginning, just like He did with John the Baptist. He is told that he is to be "prophet to the nations", a high calling indeed.

We learn from his writings that Jeremiah struggles many times with his calling. He feels totally inadequate.

> "Alas, Sovereign Lord," I said, "I do not know how to speak; I am too young".

But God simply reassures him and tells him that He will be his strength.

However, Jeremiah continues to experience much personal anguish as he seeks to carry out the Lord's purposes. He experiences rejection and persecution from among his own people. At times things seem to get too much (Jer 20:7-8):

> You deceived me, Lord, and I was deceived;
> you overpowered me and prevailed.

> I am ridiculed all day long;
>> everyone mocks me.
> Whenever I speak, I cry out
>> proclaiming violence and destruction.
> So the word of the Lord has brought me
>> insult and reproach all day long.

He reveals something very important. In the midst of his personal anguish when he reaches the point when he wants to give up, he says (Jer 20:9),

> But if I say, "I will not mention his word
>> or speak anymore in his name,"
> his word is in my heart like a fire,
>> a fire shut up in my bones.

He is aware of a fire within him. Once the call of God is in your heart, you cannot walk away from it as though it doesn't matter because deep down inside you know that God has called you. There is a fire within that cannot be quenched.

The testimony of Sacred Scripture is that God is a God who calls. This call is not limited only to particular individuals, each of us can experience a call from God.

Christian faith is based in an encounter with God

Joseph Ratzinger is one of the great theologians of our time. As Pope he wrote his first encyclical entitled *Deus caritas est*, (God is love). In that encyclical he said this:

> Being Christian is not a result of an ethical choice or a lofty idea but an encounter with an event, a person which gives life a new

horizon and a decisive direction.

Being a Christian is grounded in a moment when God touches our lives and calls us to Himself. What occurred to Abram, Moses, Isaiah and Jeremiah is actually at the base of each of us being a Christian.

There are moments, which we may be acutely aware of or perhaps not, where God has touched our lives and drawn us into his plans and purposes for us.

Being Christian is not just accepting a set of beliefs or following a moral code, ultimately it is about the experience of the person of God. When this happens, we see life differently. We are drawn to new ways of living that we didn't think was possible. Christianity according to Pope Benedict is about an encounter, a personal encounter with God in Christ.

Every one of us has had an encounter in one way or another. This is what we will explore in the coming chapters.

It is worth noting that Christianity is not about our search for God, it"s about God's search for us. As the Lord said (Jn 15:16),

> You didn't choose me, but I chose you.

Question for personal reflection:

Can I identify a moment when I felt God call me?

2

Encounter with Jesus

Who was the first disciple of Jesus once he began his public ministry? To answer this question, we can turn to the opening chapter of John's Gospel (Jn 1:35-40). There we read:

> The next day John was there again with two of his disciples. When he saw Jesus passing by, he said, "Look, the Lamb of God!" When the two disciples heard him say this, they followed Jesus. Turning around, Jesus saw them following and asked, "What do you want?" They said, "Rabbi" (which means "Teacher"), "where are you staying?" "Come," he replied, "and you will see." So they went and saw where he was staying, and they spent that day with him. It was about four in the afternoon. Andrew, Simon Peter's brother, was one of the two who heard what John had said and who had followed Jesus.

In the next verse we learn the identity of one of those two disciples of John the Baptist who followed Jesus.

> Andrew, Simon Peter's brother, was one of the two who heard what John had said and who had followed Jesus.

John identifies him and then speaks of what he immediately does once he is convinced that this Jesus of Nazareth is the Messiah that John the Baptist had been constantly speaking about:

> The first thing Andrew did was to find his brother Simon and tell him, "We have found the Messiah" (that is, the Christ). And he brought him to Jesus.

There is sense of excitement as Andrew discovers that Jesus is the person that John the Baptist had been talking about. He cannot hold this discovery to himself and sets off straight away to tell his brother, Simon. Then, as we see, Andrew brings Simon to meet the Lord.

A personal encounter with Christ

By looking at some other examples from the Gospels we will explore what happens when people encounter Christ and the change that takes place in their life. Such encounters reflect what Pope Benedict describes as the heart of being a Christian which we spoke on in the previous chapter. The words are worth reading again.

> Being Christian is not a result of an ethical choice or a lofty idea but an encounter with an event, a person which gives life a new horizon and a decisive direction.

Andrew encountered Jesus, it gave his life a whole new direction and he became a disciple of Jesus, later he was chosen as an apostle.

John's gospel has a number of examples of people encountering Jesus and the effect that this has on them.

In John, chapter four, there is the story of the encounter between Jesus and the Samaritan woman at the well. John presents the encounter in a good deal of detail. We note that there is a general conversation about matters of religion but then Jesus takes their conversation down a very interesting path. He raises a very delicate matter in relation to her life, particularly her marital status.

> He told her, "Go, call your husband and come back." "I have no husband," she replied. Jesus said to her, "You are right when you say you have no husband. The fact is, you have had five husbands, and the man you now have is not your husband. What you have just said is quite true."

We note that the woman did not take offence at this intrusion into her private life. Maybe it was because she was intrigued by Jesus and an element of trust and openness that had been established by the conversation to date. Or maybe it was the way in which Jesus spoke to her - in a loving way as opposed to a condemning and judgemental way. Whatever it was the truth Jesus spoke touched her heart and she was able to receive it and in so doing she was deeply affected. It appears that this truth telling was a means by which she was set free.

Afterwards, the woman goes into town,

> Then, leaving her water jar, the woman went back to the town and said to the people, "Come, see a man who told me everything I ever did. Could this be the Messiah?" They came out of the town and made their way toward him.

She was not ashamed to tell the people. In John's Gospel Jesus commented on the fact that coming to truth is actually a freeing moment (Jn 8:31-32)

> So Jesus said to the Jews who had believed him, "If you abide in my word, you are truly my disciples, and you will know the truth, and the truth will set you free.

This woman was not ashamed to tell the people that Jesus had told her everything she ever did. The truth had set her free. Her life was profoundly changed as a result of this conversation with Jesus.

Another example is found in the story of the woman caught in adultery, also given in John's Gospel, Chapter 11. According to the Jewish law, this woman caught in the very act of committing adultery should be stoned to death. The Pharisees and Sadducees took the opportunity to try to trap Jesus by the situation. But instead, Jesus does not directly engage in answering their question but starts writing on the sand instead. John describes it,

> But Jesus bent down and started to write on the ground with his finger. When they kept on questioning him, he straightened up and said to them, "Let any one of you who is without sin be the first to throw a stone at her." Again he stooped down and wrote on the ground.

John records that the crowd melted away and Jesus was left alone with the woman. Then we are told,

> Jesus straightened up and asked her, "Woman, where are they? Has no one condemned you?" "No one, sir," she said. "Then neither do I condemn you," Jesus declared. "Go now and sin no more."

Here we find a beautiful act of mercy which must have overwhelmed the woman. Not only did this woman feel relief that she was not to be stoned to death, but more than that Jesus words would have sunk deep into her heart. We sense that she would have reformed her life.

People can get locked into a sense of their own worthlessness and in a particular pattern to their life that have led them down a particular destructive path. When life seems to be taking a course we can think that all is inevitable. People sense that they have messed up their lives and there is nothing that can change this.

People can have the sense of being a hopeless failure because of their past history. They can feel that they have no future and their destiny is determined. However, just like this woman who committed adultery, her destiny was changed in a moment when Jesus said the words "Neither do I condemn you".

When Jesus said to her not to sin anymore one senses that she was set free from her past. She could now live a new life. She could change. This story reminds us that we are not determined by what has happened to us. Jesus has the capacity to transform a person's life.

Another example of how a person's life was dramatically changed through their personal encounter with Jesus is the story given by John of the woman who came to the Pharisee's house and began to wash the feet of Jesus with her tears and wiped them dry with her hair.

St Luke records this incident (7:36-50). What is important to note is Jesus' comment to his host, Simon the Pharisee:

> I tell you that her many sins are forgiven, so she showed great love. But the person who is forgiven only a little will love only a little." Then Jesus said to her, "Your sins are forgiven."

At some point her encounter with Jesus led to a profound conversion for which she is deeply grateful.

These stories show us the power of what happens when there is an encounter with Jesus.

Let us briefly consider one more example of an encounter with Jesus that led to a radical change in a person's life: the story of Matthew, the tax collector, who responded immediately when Jesus said to him "Follow me." There would have been a back story to this which we have not been given. We do not know what it was that prompted Matthew to abandon his old way of life, but he did.

We are then told that after this change to his life he throws a party. This party is a celebration of the new life he has chosen and marks the end of his previous way of life. It is a celebration of a man who has come to know that he has been set free. Jesus impacted his life so much that he decided to leave everything aside – he chose to make a radical redirection of his life. And he did this joyfully.

Jesus brings about conversion and new life

Jesus came for the people who are struggling. It is the ones whose lives are not together that Jesus wanted to spend his time with. He is willing to talk to the Samaritan woman at the well and speaks a word of truth to her. He shows mercy to the woman who committed adultery. Jesus relates to ordinary people with all their various struggles. They are the ones that Jesus wants to engage with. People's hearts are changed, all sorts of things start to be good about their lives that were not good with their lives before.

John wrote in his first letter (I Jn 1:1-2),

> That which was from the beginning, which we have heard, which we have seen with our eyes, which we have looked at and our hands have touched—this we proclaim concerning the Word of life. The life appeared; we have seen it and testify to it, and we proclaim to you the eternal life, which was with the Father and has appeared to us.

This passage reveals the experience of the Apostle John - that meeting the Lord has given him life. Faith brings us to life, to richness and fullness of life.

This new life found by encountering Jesus is one that has the quality of joy. Pope Francis, in his first Apostolic Exhortation, *Evangelii Gaudium*, stated,

> The joy of the gospel fills the hearts and the lives of all who encounter Jesus. Those who accept his offer of salvation are set free from sin, sorrow, inner emptiness and loneliness.

Encounter with Jesus changes our lives. This change is a change that brings joy to our lives

Question for personal reflection:

What has your encounter with Jesus brought to your life?

3

The experience of healing

Healing people from all sorts of diseases and sicknesses, even raising the dead, was a very significant aspect of the public ministry of Jesus.

The healing of a leper reveals not only Jesus' power to heal, but also the motivation in the heart of Jesus to heal those who were suffering. It is described by Matthew (8:1-4).

> When Jesus came down from the mountainside, large crowds followed him. A man with leprosy came and knelt before him and said, "Lord, if you are willing, you can make me clean." Jesus reached out his hand and touched the man. "I am willing," he said. "Be clean!" Immediately he was cleansed of his leprosy. Then Jesus said to him, "See that you don't tell anyone. But go, show yourself to the priest and offer the gift Moses commanded, as a testimony to them

In Israel during that time, one would not dare touch a leper. It was considered to be a very contagious disease. Similar to the way in which Covid-19 impacted society when we were urged to keep a distance with people around us. There was much fear about catching leprosy by touching someone with the disease. Yet, Jesus' immediate response was to put out his hand and touch the leper.

In the Jerusalem Bible's translation, it says that "Of course I want to be cured." That reflects a central truth behind the healing ministry of Jesus: He wants to heal. A request for a miracle is not an imposition on him, nor is it something He feels that He should do but rather it is something that flows from Jesus' heart. Jesus wants to heal.

Across the gospels, there are over 25 accounts of specific miracles of healing. But there were many more. Not every miracle was recorded. We are told of occasions when there were large numbers of people being healed.

Each of these individual accounts has a human touch to it. There is an interaction between the person and Jesus. The miracle is not just the physical healing, but the effect that this has on the person healed, on their life and on their faith.

Another example of a miracle is in the following chapter of Matthew's gospel (9:18-26). We read,

> While he was saying this, a synagogue leader came and knelt before him and said, "My daughter has just died. But come and put your hand on her, and she will live." Jesus got up and went with him, and so did his disciples. Just then a woman who had been subject to bleeding for twelve years came up behind him and touched the edge of his cloak. She said to herself, "If I only touch his cloak, I will be healed." Jesus turned and saw her. "Take heart, daughter," he said, "your faith has healed you." And the woman was healed at that moment. When Jesus entered the synagogue leader's house and saw the noisy crowd and people playing pipes, he said, "Go away. The girl is not

> dead but asleep." But they laughed at him. After the crowd had been put outside, he went in and took the girl by the hand, and she got up. News of this spread through all that region.

Firstly, we note that there is a miracle within a miracle. A ruler has come up to Jesus and said to him "my daughter just died, but you can bring her back to life." While that is extraordinary in itself (bringing someone back to life), it is the miracle that happens in the midst of the story that is also interesting. It is described simply here – Jesus is moving through the town and a woman who has suffered from a haemorrhage for 12 years just wanted to touch the hem of Jesus' garment.

When Jesus identifies her he says, "Take heart my daughter, your faith has made you well." The woman, despite the suffering she was experiencing, was driven by her faith. She was convinced that if only she could touch the hem of his garment she would be healed. It was almost an insignificant thing to just touch the hem of the garment. She wanted to be anonymous and did not presume to ask or seek his attention. Her heart was driven by a faith and confidence that Jesus could heal her just simply by touching the hem of his garment. And Jesus acknowledges the fact that it was her faith that made her well.

Jesus commented on several occasions that it was faith that saved the sick person. Healings come about because of the faith of the person who believes that they can be healed. Faith is the key element in healing. When there is faith, one believes, one asks and one receives. If there is no faith, one does not ask and one does not receive. Faith is critical to healing.

Healing ministry continued through the Church

The healing ministry of Jesus continues in the life of the early church. From the Acts of the Apostles (3:1-10) we read that Peter and John were going up to the temple to pray and they saw a cripple begging at the door. Acts tells us of the response of these two Apostles,

> Then Peter said, "Silver or gold I do not have, but what I do have I give you. In the name of Jesus Christ of Nazareth, walk." Taking him by the right hand, he helped him up, and instantly the man's feet and ankles became strong. He jumped to his feet and began to walk. Then he went with them into the temple courts, walking and jumping, and praising God.

Peter proclaimed "In the name of Jesus Christ of Nazareth, walk". The cripple then stood up and was able to walk. Peter is conscious that he does not have the power to heal the cripple, but readily acknowledges that that the power is from Jesus. Peter knows that he can invoke that healing power.

This has been evident throughout the life of the church. There are many occasions of healings taking place over the course of Christian history. Healing has been associated with the life and ministry of many saints.

Let us consider on example: St André Bessett, who became known as "the miracle man of Montreal". He belonged to the Congregation of the Holy Cross, but due to frail health it was decided that he would not become a priest but was made a lay brother instead. One of his tasks was to be the doorkeeper at a house of the Congregation in Montreal and he did it for forty years.

He had a great devotion to St Joseph and would pray for the people that came to talk to him as the doorkeeper. People experienced miracles of healing and this grew over the next forty years. He had thousands of people who contacted him to ask him to intercede for them for a healing.

There are over 100,000 miracles connected with St André Bessett. In his later years he received over 80,000 letter requests per year for his prayers. He always acknowledged that this was the power of God mediated through St Joseph. In 1937, when he died, over a million people were at his funeral.

This is just one story of one saint and it can be multiplied. In the Church if a saint is to be considered for canonisation there has to be a miracle associated with them.

However, it is not only saints who are instruments of healing, but also there are many places that are famous for being places of healing. The best known for Catholics is in Lourdes, France. In 1858 Our Lady appeared to St Bernadette by a grotto and she told her to dig the ground and a small stream of water started to flow out. Very soon there were miracles associated with these healing waters. Today, millions of people a year travel to Lourdes to bathe in its healing waters.

A story of healing

One example of a healing that took place at Lourdes is that of Julianna Eliarde. Julianna recounted that at the age of 28 years old she suffered from "Regional Pain Syndrome". Her excruciating pain confined her to a wheelchair for eight years. Fifty specialists were unable to help her and her leg was dying and at risk of amputation. Three years into her illness, she decided to turn back to God and started praying the Chaplet of the Divine Mercy. She then made a general confession.

She felt transformed and started to pray three hours a day, and went to weekly adoration. She prayed for a spiritual healing first and then for physical healing and to accept the possible loss of her leg. In 2008, against doctor's advice, she went on a pilgrimage to Lourdes and went to the Eucharistic Benediction. When the priest lifted the monstrance, she felt a pain like an electric current running through her leg that lasted several minutes. She then felt the need to go to the grotto and pray the rosary. While she was praying she was captivated by a tiny light in the sky and felt that Mary was behind the light. She then heard the words in her heart that said "Julie don't worry, everything will be all right, just trust". She was immediately overwhelmed by the love of Mother Mary. She felt she had a relationship with her heavenly mother that she never felt before. She realised she had no pain in her leg and asked for assistance to get up from her wheelchair. She was able to bear weight on her leg and she was able to walk.

This is an extraordinary story of not only a physical healing but also a total transformation of her heart. Her faith led her to go to Lourdes, and filled her with such love and gratitude towards God. Healings concern the experience of the love and mercy of God, such that the person healed is completely transformed in their relationship with God.

Healings reveal the heart of God towards suffering humanity. Healings reveal the depth of mercy in the heart of God towards all who are burdened with suffering. Healings reveal the true nature of God in a way that can never be understood conceptually or intellectually. Healing not only touches the body but transforms the heart and the soul.

Over the years of my priesthood I have had occasions when I witnessed the healing power of God. One example of this what when I was a priest at The Entrance Parish in the Central Coast of NSW. On a Sunday I preached on a healing miracle of Jesus and decided at the end of Mass that I would stay on the altar and offered to pray over people. Many came forward and I prayed over many people for some time after the Mass.

A year later, I was celebrating Sunday Mass and after Mass as I stood outside the Church talking to people, a couple waited to speak with me. This couple said that they were at the Mass during a holiday the previous year and came forward for healing as they were unable to have a child and the doctors had given up. He then introduced his wife and their three-month-old baby.

Miracles do happen and God continues to heal. The Scriptures reveal this, the tradition of the Church testifies to this, particularly in the lives of saints and special places like Lourdes. Miracles continue to happen.

Question for personal reflection:

Can you describe an experience where you are convinced that you experienced the healing power of God?

4

Bringing about Conversion

A question I like to pose to people is: "In ten words or less what is the essential message that Jesus wanted to convey in the Gospel?" I receive many different responses, like "love one another", all correct in their own way, but not, I believe, penetrating to the heart of the proclamation of Jesus.

The best way I would recommend is to look for an answer to this question by considering the original proclamation that Jesus gave when he started his public ministry. Normally when someone begins something, they usually state their fundamental message and purpose in the beginning. Along the way they may fill it out with more information and give further expression to their central theme and purpose.

Thus, to answer this question, we can turn to the opening chapter of St Mark's Gospel (1:14–15):

> After John was put in prison, Jesus went into Galilee, proclaiming the good news of God. "The time has come," he said. "The kingdom of God has come near. Repent and believe the good news!"

This very succinct expression of what Jesus' opening message was does capture what his whole purpose was about. He says that the "time has come". God has become man and entered human history definitively with the Incarnation. The time of waiting is over, now God is acting definitively.

Jesus says that the "kingdom of God is close at hand". This means that now one can come into a relationship with God and come under the power and saving mercy of God. Jesus was to bring the kingdom of his Father, break the power of darkness and evil and death by his own saving death and resurrection. God's work of salvation has now come upon humanity.

Then, we note that Jesus calls for a response to this proclamation. It is expressed, again, very succinctly: "repent and believe". The word "repent" can make people feel uncomfortable. It can sound like harsh and judgemental. It can be off-putting.

However, when looking at the origin of the word we can get a clearer understanding of what the Lord is calling for. The word is derived from the Greek word, *metanoia*, and actually means a change of direction, a re-orientation, a transformation of one's life to see things in a new way.

This understanding can help us understand what Jesus is saying. Jesus is saying: this is a definitive moment in history where God is going to do a great work of salvation and people need to re-adjust and turn away from the things that pre-occupy them and focus on what God is doing instead.

Examples of *Metanoia*

An example of this change of direction in one's life is the story of Zacchaeus, given in St Luke's Gospel (19:1-10):

> Jesus entered Jericho and was passing through. A man was there by the name of Zacchaeus; he was a chief tax collector and was wealthy. He wanted to see who Jesus was, but because he was short he could not see over the crowd. So he ran ahead and climbed a sycamore-fig tree to see him, since Jesus was coming that way. When Jesus reached the spot, he looked up and said to him, "Zacchaeus, come down immediately. I must stay at your house today." So he came down at once and welcomed him gladly. All the people saw this and began to mutter, "He has gone to be the guest of a sinner." But Zacchaeus stood up and said to the Lord, "Look, Lord! Here and now I give half of my possessions to the poor, and if I have cheated anybody out of anything, I will pay back four times the amount." Jesus said to him, "Today salvation has come to this house, because this man, too, is a son of Abraham. For the Son of Man came to seek and to save the lost."

Jesus saw an opportunity when he noticed Zacchaeus up in the tree. Why did Jesus choose Zacchaeus? We don't know. But Jesus saw an opportunity to bring a man who was curious about him to conversion.

We notice that Jesus did not lecture or correct Zacchaeus about his wrong doings, but simply showed interest in him. And that brought about the extraordinary transformation in Zacchaeus. At the meal Zacchaeus makes a bold announcement that he is going to radically change his life: "Behold, Lord, the half of my goods I give to the poor; and if I have defrauded anyone of anything, I restore it fourfold." Somehow the encounter he had with Jesus so affected him that he no longer wanted to live the way he did before.

The comment that Jesus makes is indicative of his ultimate purpose: "Today, salvation has come to this house, since he also is the son of Abraham. For the Son of man came to seek and to save the lost."

The transformation that took place in Zacchaeus is what happens when people encounter Christ. People are not told how to change, they are not being corrected and told what they are doing wrong, but their encounter with Jesus leads them to want to change and be different. This is not borne out of an imposition but instead they are responding to an experience of Christ whereby they want to change their ways.

A life recalibrated

A man that I have known and admired for many years is Robert Falzon. Robert willingly tells the story of his own journey of faith. He says that when he has looked back on his life he recognises that there have been several moments of conversion.

When he was seventeen, he felt God was calling him and thought that God wanted him to become a priest. But this was not the case. He then joined a Catholic group in Brisbane and eventually met his wife there and they got married. He was twenty-seven.

Robert then started a small business and was very successful in it. This consumed him to the point where he would often neglect his family as he was away on trips for the business.

In 1997 he had another encounter with the Lord. He went on a retreat to the US and the leader of the conference said to the audience "Are you going to continue to deal for dollars or will you deal for destinies?" Robert felt as though the leader was speaking just to him. This statement shook him and changed him. After much prayer and discernment, he decided to sell his business and changed the way he lived.

With the help of some other Christian men he started a ministry called "Men Alive". Robert realigned, recalibrated and reoriented his life. God showed him a new perspective, a way to look at the world and a way to look at what he was called to do. God changed him, then called him and sent him.

Over the last twenty years, Men Alive have run 500 missions to 35,000 men in Australia. God has worked in the men in they have worked with in parishes and in schools and continues to work in this ministry to this day. He recognises that God constantly realigns his life and still calls him to turn his gaze back to Him. He says, "The process of life conversion over the whole of life is an essential journey of discipleship and interior growth. Open your heart for the conversion and be realigned with Christ whenever He calls you."

The Christian life is about these moments when God calls. It is about moments where there is a call to redirect one"s life and purpose. The Christian life is about allowing an ongoing conversion. It is not an imposition upon oneself. It is hearing something that draws a person forward and God is in the midst of what the person is being asked to do.

Humility as the ground for conversion

In a parable given St Luke 18:9-14, the Lord is contrasting two figures – one is self-satisfied and not open to conversion, the other is only too aware of their failings and seeks conversion.

> To some who were confident of their own righteousness and looked down on everyone else, Jesus told this parable: Two men went up to the temple to pray, one a Pharisee and the other a tax collector. The Pharisee stood by himself and prayed: "God, I thank you that I am not like other people—robbers, evildoers, adulterers—or even like this tax collector. I fast twice a week and give a tenth of all I get." But the tax collector stood at a distance. He would not even look up to heaven, but beat his breast and said, "God, have mercy on me, a sinner." I tell you that this man, rather than the other, went home justified before God. For all those who exalt themselves will be humbled, and those who humble themselves will be exalted.

This parable reminds us of what lies at the heart of conversion. The Pharisee was talking only about himself and how good he was and how he was doing good things for God. The tax collector, on the other hand, was asking for mercy and recognised his fundamental need. God accepted the prayer of the tax collector.

One of the important elements of conversion is the recognition that one does not have to have everything all together. Humility is foundational to coming to conversion. God can really work with a humble, contrite soul.

This parable had a strong influence with the desert monks residing in Egypt, Palestine and Syria. The importance of a humble and contrite heart and the scriptural injunction to "pray constantly" (I Thess 5:16) led to a tradition of prayer whereby the monks repeated continuously, "Lord, be merciful to me a sinner".

This approach to prayer continued to find expression particularly in the Eastern church; being promoted within the Byzantine Church, it eventually spread to Russia. The monks realised that the repetition of the simple prayer softened the heart to accept the saving action of Grace. It is now commonly called the "Jesus Prayer".

By saying this prayer, the monks were conscious of the words and the meaning of the words – recognising one's true condition (a sinner) and by constantly saying the prayer this disposition of humble need for God takes possession of the heart. Now a person surrenders their need for mercy and salvation into the hands of God. Thus, one is disposed to conversion.

"Pray for my conversion"

On a trip to Calabria in Italy some years back, I was privileged to visit a Carthusian monastery. The Carthusian order was founded by St Bruno originally in Germany. The monks live a penitential life devoted to prayer and solitude but live within a communal setting. A monk in his early thirties showed me around and when the time came for me to leave, the monk said to me, "Pray for my conversion".

His words struck me. Here was a monk who has devoted his life to prayer and poverty yet wanted prayer for his conversion. This monk knew a basic truth: that the Christian life is about constantly seeking conversion. The Christian life rests in an openness to God so God can shape and form us. This is not a matter of pressure to be better as simply allowing grace to move in such a way that we are drawn closer to Christ.

One final comment on the call to conversion. In his account of the crucifixion Luke recounts an incident between Jesus and the two thieves crucified with him (23:39-43). We read:

> One of the criminals who hung there hurled insults at him: "Aren't you the Messiah? Save yourself and us!" But the other criminal rebuked him. "Don't you fear God," he said, "since you are under the same sentence? We are punished justly, for we are getting what our deeds deserve. But this man has done nothing wrong." Then he said, "Jesus, remember me when you come into your kingdom." Jesus answered him, "Truly I tell you, today you will be with me in paradise."

"Jesus, remember me when you come into your Kingdom." This story shows what happens when individuals abandon themselves to the mercy of God. Jesus responds unhesitatingly and accepts his request completely and totally. One of the wonderful things about conversion is the fact that God completely and totally forgives. Jesus saw into the heart of this dying criminal. Conversion, in the end, is so profoundly simple. It is really just the moment wherein one surrenders to God and puts all one's trust completely and totally in God. And God responds to such a request.

Question for personal reflection:

Can I identify a moment when I felt a call to conversion as a realignment of my life?

5

Encountering the glory of the Lord

As we have noted, Pope Benedict wrote in his first encyclical entitled *Deus caritas est*, "God is love":

> Being Christian is not a result of an ethical choice or a lofty idea but an encounter with an event, a person which gives life a new horizon and a decisive direction.

Pope Benedict understood that contemporary society will only come to faith through an individual and personal encounter with Jesus Christ. During his relatively short pontificate he wrote a three-volume work entitled, "Jesus of Nazareth".

In the first volume the Pope explains his purpose commenting,

> The disciple who walks with Jesus is caught up with him into communion with God.

Here he reminds us that we are to be disciples attentive to Jesus on a daily basis and this will, in turn, lead us into a more profound relationship with God.

His approach in these books is to invite the reader to observe and listen to Jesus. In his own words, to have a personal encounter with Jesus.

In the chapters so far we have looked at what has happened to people who have encountered the Lord. We looked at some Old Testament examples of people called by God. Then we looked at some New Testament stories of people who had an encounter with Christ and the way that this encounter radically changed the orientation of their lives. As Pope Benedict reminded us, the encounter with Christ opens us to experience God Himself.

In the final book of the Bible, the Book of Revelation, we are presented with a number of mystical experiences of the Apostle John. Chapter 4 of the Book of Revelations begins with these words,

> After this I looked, and there before me was a door standing open in heaven. And the voice I had first heard speaking to me like a trumpet said, "Come up here, and I will show you what must take place after this."

John was given a vision of heaven. In this mystical vision he is shown the glory of God. He describes what is essentially indescribable in these words,

> At once I was in the Spirit, and there before me was a throne in heaven with someone sitting on it. And the one who sat there had the appearance of jasper and ruby. A rainbow that shone like an emerald encircled the throne. Surrounding the throne were twenty-four other thrones, and seated on them were twenty-four elders. They were dressed in white and had crowns of gold on their heads. From the throne came flashes of lightning, rumblings and peals of thunder. In front of the throne, seven lamps were blazing. These are the seven spirits of God. Also in front of the throne there was what

looked like a sea of glass, clear as crystal.

He is then conscious of the worship of God taking place:

> Day and night they never stop saying: "Holy, holy, holy is the Lord God Almighty, who was, and is, and is to come."

This experience is similar to what the prophet Isaiah experienced as he prayed in the temple (see Is 6:1-4). The angels around the throne cried out,

> "Holy, holy, holy is the Lord Almighty. the whole earth is full of his glory."

We Catholics are familiar with these words. We are invited to join the angels and saints in their song of worship at every Mass. The priest, in the dialogue and the Preface before the Eucharistic Prayer, invites the congregation at the Mass to unite with the voices of angels in heaven who gaze upon the heavenly glory of God. As we prepare for the Eucharistic Prayer the priest invites the congregation to "Life up your hearts", and we respond, "we lift them up to the Lord". This is the moment where we can lift our gaze up towards God and lift our hearts in worship of God. We sing the song of the angels, the *Sanctus* (Holy, Holy, Holy Lord).

At this moment, heaven and earth are united and there is one hymn of praise for God issuing forth. The whole church, whenever it sings the *Sanctus*, is united with the worship of God in heaven.

Experience of the glory of the Lord

In the account of the Transfiguration of the Lord in the Gospels we read of a unique experience of Jesus' three closest disciples. St Matthew (17:1-9) tells us:

> After six days Jesus took with him Peter, James and John the brother of James, and led them up a high mountain by themselves. There he was transfigured before them. His face shone like the sun, and his clothes became as white as the light. Just then there appeared before them Moses and Elijah, talking with Jesus. Peter said to Jesus, "Lord, it is good for us to be here. If you wish, I will put up three shelters—one for you, one for Moses and one for Elijah." While he was still speaking, a bright cloud covered them, and a voice from the cloud said, "This is my Son, whom I love; with him I am well pleased. Listen to him!" When the disciples heard this, they fell facedown to the ground, terrified. But Jesus came and touched them. "Get up," he said. "Don't be afraid." When they looked up, they saw no one except Jesus.

St Matthew speaks of, "after six days", what happened six days before the Transfiguration took place? In the previous chapter we read that, six days earlier, Jesus asked his disciples about his identity. He asks them, "Who do you say I am?" (Mt 16:15). Simon Peter replied,

> You are the Christ, the Son of the living God.

And Jesus answered him,

> Blessed are you, Simon Bar-Jona! For flesh and blood has not revealed this to you, but my Father who is in heaven. And I tell you, you are Peter, and on this rock I will build my Church, and the powers of death shall not prevail against it. I will give you the keys of the kingdom of heaven.

In that moment Jesus reveals what his long-term plan and purpose is going to be – establishing the Church. It can be built on a solid foundation of the faith of Peter and the other disciples. Because Peter was able to make such a clear declaration of faith, Jesus could say that he was now ready to be the rock on which he was to build his Church.

However, immediately after this he speaks of suffering and dying at the hands of the elders and chief priests. Peter objects and Jesus rebukes him:

> Get behind me Satan! You are a hindrance to me; for you are not on the side of God, but of men.

This is an important background to the account of the Transfiguration. This experience was firstly a profound confirming experience for the three chosen disciples. It is to be understood in the light of the Lord's passion, death and ultimately his resurrection. It is a special grace that was given to them to prepare them for what was ahead. It is interesting that coming down from the mountain, Jesus commands them not to tell anyone about the vision, until the Son of Man is raised from the dead. This was a special gift given to the disciples to hold on to.

For the three chosen disciples this is a moment of the experience of the glory of the Lord. These experiences of the presence of God, the glory of God, the power and majesty of God are given to various people like Isaiah, John, Peter, James and John on the mountain wherein God's presence is revealed and wherein one gets a glimpse of the glory and majesty of God.

Experience of Adoration of Blessed Sacrament

However, such moments of the glory of the Lord can occur to us as well. During the World Youth Day (WYD) in Sydney in 2008 I was talking to young people about their experiences. I spoke to a young girl who shared that she had been Catholic but had not been practicing her faith. During the WYD, Adoration tents had been set up around the city where the Blessed Sacrament was exposed and young people could come to pray.

This girl was curious and so she went into the tent to see what was happening and while she knelt she was so overwhelmed by the experience that she began to cry. She was so overcome by the moment as she felt the presence of God in the Blessed Sacrament. In that instant her faith came alive. She had her own version of the Transfiguration in that tent.

One of the ways wherein one experiences the presence of the Lord is during the Holy Eucharist, or during a time of Adoration.

Sean shared an experience of his. In 2008, in Sri Lanka, Sean asked his boss who was quite a dictatorial person if he could start going to Adoration during his lunch hour as it was the start of the Lenten season. Surprisingly, his boss agreed to let him go. Despite hearing discouraging comments from his boss, Sean continued to attend Adoration during his lunch break.

About a week into this, his boss asked him what he did when he went to church in his lunch hour. He asked if anyone could go (as he himself was Buddhist), so Sean said he would take him the next day. They went to Adoration and after his first time, his boss said that there was something there and chose to come again the following day.

After about three weeks his boss came out of Adoration looking shell-shocked and Sean asked him what happened? And his boss told him that during Adoration that day, he saw the face of Jesus in the Blessed Sacrament. His boss then began to change his ways, he turned away from witchcraft (which is something he used to dabble in), started to read the Bible and developed a prayer life and listened to recordings of prayer meetings. A few years later, Sean heard that he was baptised into the Catholic faith.

The Jesus we believe in is the historical Jesus of 2,000 years ago but He is also the risen Lord who lives now and is present in the Blessed Sacrament. Stories like these are signs that His presence is very real. The risen Lord appeared to his disciples on a number of occasions. These appearances were to reveal his risen glory to his disciples. The Gospel that the Apostles proclaimed was that Jesus not only died but rose from the dead.

The story of the two disciples on the road to Emmaus expresses clearly the intention of the risen Lord to reveal himself to his disciples. We are told that the two disciples on the road to

Emmaus were down-hearted and confused, feeling lost. Jesus comes up and walks by their side and starts a conversation with them but they did not recognise him.

Later, after they realised that it was Jesus who accompanied them, they commented,

> Did not our hearts burn within us while he talked to us on the road, while he opened to us the Scriptures?

There was something in that conversation that was touching their spirit. They recognised Jesus in the "breaking of the bread", the Eucharist. This is where we meet and know the Lord now - in the Holy Eucharist, in receiving Holy Communion, and also when one kneels in adoration before Him in the Blessed Sacrament.

Question for personal reflection:

Can you recall a time when you sensed the presence of the Lord – in prayer, in reading Sacred Scripture, in the Mass, receiving Holy Communion, in times of adoration?

Module Two
Head: Our Identity as Christians

6

The Four Truths

The first module explored what happens in the human heart when a person truly encounters Christ. In this second module we will explore our identity as Christians. There are some key fundamentals to being a Christian. To understand who we are as Christians provides the impetus to draw others to know and love Christ. It helps us understand what is involved in the process of coming to faith in Christ.

Following a Synod held in Rome which focused on young people, Pope Francis, in 2019, produced an Apostolic Exhortation addressed to young people. It was entitled, *Christus Vivit* (Christ Lives). In the document the Pope presents what he considers four very important truths for young people. These truths are important for young people to understand, and they are important for all Christians. They are the key foundations to the Christian life. The Pope described them in this way:

> God loves you,
> Christ saves you,
> He is alive,

The Spirit gives life

We will explore each of these "four truths" in some detail in the coming chapters.

We will commence with the first one – "God loves you".

"God loves you" is a commonly known and frequently used phrase, and something that can be passed over as self-evident as it is a phrase that is so well known. We can miss absorbing its full meaning and significance. While it is something that is familiar and used commonly, it is a profound revelation about the nature of God and the nature of our relationship with God. God is love and our relationship with Him is grounded in love.

God's self-revelation

Earlier we considered the call of Moses. The Book of Exodus, Chapter 3, records Moses' encounter with God at the foot of Mount Horeb (or Sinai). God manifests His presence in the burning bush. Let us recall the setting.

> Now Moses was tending the flock of Jethro his father-in-law, the priest of Midian, and he led the flock to the far side of the wilderness and came to Horeb, the mountain of God. There the angel of the Lord appeared to him in flames of fire from within a bush. Moses saw that though the bush was on fire it did not burn up. So Moses thought, "I will go over and see this strange sight—why the bush does not burn up."

God identifies Himself to Moses in these words,

> "I am the God of your father, the God of Abraham, the God of Isaac and the God of Jacob."

God simply identifies Himself as the God known to Moses' ancestors. While Moses accepts this identification, he seeks to know more about the character of the God who has called him and whose purposes he now serves. Following the escape (the Exodus) from Egypt and once again in the shadow of the holy mountain, Horeb, or Sinai, Moses pursues his personal search to know more fully the identity of God. Thus, in Exodus 33:18 he asks God to reveal Himself to him. He asks, rather boldly,

> "Now show me your glory."

And God agrees to do this and says He will pass before him. God's glory is such that a human being cannot behold His glory "face to face". He advises Moses to stay behind the cleft of a rock and said He will pass and put His hand across Moses as He passes by as the intensity of God's glory is too much for Moses to actually see Him. Moses has this moment when God reveals His glory on the mountain, even if God was still hidden from him face to face.

> And the Lord said, "I will cause all my goodness to pass in front of you, and I will proclaim my name, the Lord, in your presence. I will have mercy on whom I will have mercy, and I will have compassion on whom I will have compassion. But," he said, "you cannot see my face, for no one may see me and live." Then the Lord said, "There is a place near me where you may stand on a rock. When my glory passes by, I will put you in a cleft in the

rock and cover you with my hand until I have passed by. Then I will remove my hand and you will see my back; but my face must not be seen."

This is a very significant grace given to Moses. But there is more to come. In the following chapter God offers a further revelation of His nature. It is described in these words,

> And he passed in front of Moses, proclaiming, "The Lord, the Lord, the compassionate and gracious God, slow to anger, abounding in love and faithfulness".

This is a very significant moment of revelation as God describes the qualities of His character. He is a God of love, of compassion, of faithfulness. It is an extraordinary moment of self-disclosure. Here we see God offering a description of his inner nature.

Love that is constant

Let us consider two particular features of this love. We are told that it is faithful or, as some translations say, "steadfast". In other words, God's love is constant – it doesn't change. Just like the sun shining. Even if the sky is cloudy and we cannot see the sun, it is still there in the heavens. God's love is there even when we cannot see it.

In St Matthew's Gospel (5:43-48) Jesus speaks about the nature of love, the nature of love in the heart of God.

> You have heard that it was said, "Love your neighbour and hate your enemy". But I tell you, love your enemies and pray for those

> who persecute you, that you may be children of your Father in heaven. He causes his sun to rise on the evil and the good, and sends rain on the righteous and the unrighteous. If you love those who love you, what reward will you get? Are not even the tax collectors doing that? And if you greet only your own people, what are you doing more than others? Do not even pagans do that? Be perfect, therefore, as your heavenly Father is perfect.

It is true that we humans tend to separate people depending on whether they are on our side or not. There is a tendency to create division in our affections based on whether someone is within our favour or outside our favour. We offer our love to those we choose. We human beings are selective as to whom we will love.

Jesus challenges us to love our enemies. The reason he can do this is that this is what God Himself does. God loves all people irrespective of their standing with Him, constantly and steadily. God doesn't have people who are outside his favour, even if people choose to put themselves outside of His favour. God's love is constant like the sun shining or the rain falling. God doesn't pull back his love when someone doesn't treat him right. God is not like that.

This contrasts strikingly with how human beings are. When one person is offended by another, there is a tendency to withdraw love from that person. God is different. God's love is steadfast and constant, and this is the true standard of love. This is how all should love. God's love never changes. It is constant. It never changes because God never changes.

Love that is personal

God's love is a love that is personal. It is a challenge for us at times to believe that God loves me personally. We can readily accept that God loves the world and the whole of humanity but how can God's love be special, unique and particular just for me? God's love for each of us is so personal and individual that it manages to engage with each person in a very particular way. Yet God's love for each person is individual and personal. God engages with each person in an individual way. This is a wonderful and extraordinary truth.

Thus, we hear the comforting words of Jesus (Mt 11:28):

> "Come to me, all you who are weary and burdened, and I will give you rest".

An image that expresses this very poignantly is the image of the Sacred Heart. In the image that the Lord revealed to St Margaret Mary Alacoque in 1673, we see that around the heart of Jesus is a fire. His arms are stretched out wide open. Jesus made himself completely and totally welcoming.

In the revelation to St Margaret Mary Jesus said to her,

> "Behold this heart that loves humanity so much".

It is a powerful image. This heart that was pierced on Calvary, this heart has a fire of love for each person individually. Jesus invites us to come to him and discover the depth of this love.

This is the love I mean

The Gospel and Letters of John constantly speak about the love of God. John reminds us that when we come to consider the nature of love we should not look to our own personal experience of love but rather contemplate the revelation of the nature of love that is in the heart of God. In I John 4:10 the Beloved Disciple says,

> This is love: not that we loved God, but that he loved us and sent his Son as an atoning sacrifice for our sins.

John deeply knew the love of God revealed in Jesus Christ. Ultimately, we love because we have experienced love. There is no purer source of love than that which comes from God Himself.

Question for personal reflection

Can you identify a moment when you became aware of the personal love of God for you?

7

Christ saves you

Pope Francis proposed four truths to young people, truths that are relevant to all baptised Catholics. The second truth he offered to the young people is that "Christ saves you."

The question of the need to be saved is problematic for contemporary people. Many today do not see a need to be saved. In contemporary society which has advanced in technology, communications, standard of living and development of medicines and so forth, there is a sense of confidence that people have that they need to be able to manage by themselves. In an age that promotes individualism and the pursuit of one's own personal goals, many do not consider that they need help, or feel that it is all up to them. They see that they must set out in life to be the "best version of themselves". There is the constant promotion of the notion of resilience, which suggests that we can create our own personal future. Many today believe that our destiny is up to ourselves.

Pelagianism

In the fourth century there was an English priest living in Rome by the name of Pelagius. He was convinced that people could manage their own lives by themselves with a bit of guidance through education and the exercise of their willpower. St Augustine of Hippo, North Africa, was very concerned about this and wrote strongly against the views of Pelagius. St Augustine understood that Christianity is founded on the saving action of Christ. If we can save ourselves then why would Christ come and die on the cross? St Augustine wrote very eloquently about the fact that every person needs the saving grace of God.

Recently, Pope Francis spoke about the dangers of Pelagianism in the modern world (see *Gaudete et Exultate*, 47-62). Speaking to Catholics who are susceptible to this tendency he says,

> Those who yield to this pelagian or semi-pelagian mindset, even though they speak warmly of God's grace, ultimately trust only in their own powers and feel superior to others because they observe certain rules or remain intransigently faithful to a particular Catholic style.

He adds later drawing on the consistent teaching of the Fathers of the Church,

> The Church has repeatedly taught that we are justified not by our own works or efforts, but by the grace of the Lord, who always takes the initiative. The Fathers of the Church, even before Saint Augustine, clearly expressed this fundamental belief. Saint John Chrysostom said that God pours into us the very source of all his gifts even before we enter into battle. Saint

> Basil the Great remarked that the faithful glory in God alone, for "they realize that they lack true justice and are justified only through faith in Christ".

Pelagianism is alive and well in the world today. In Christian circles, people have the idea that one gets to heaven by doing good works and, having done enough of them, presume that they will be entitled to entry into heaven. Again, this raises the question, why did Christ die on the cross, if we can earn heaven by our good works? This is a very important question to consider.

As a young priest I had a parish youth group in my first parish. One Sunday evening a young man who took me aside after a presentation on the need to be saved and said that he did not agree with what I had said. He did not believe he needed to be saved.

The following weekend this same young man was body surfing and got caught in a rip and was swept out to sea. He was quite athletic and was a capable swimmer, but he was struggling to swim against the rip and finally put his hands up to have the lifesavers come and rescue him.

The following Sunday, this same man sheepishly came up to me and said he understood what it meant to be saved. Although he was strong enough to swim as he was young, fit and healthy, he needed someone to save him as the rip was stronger than his capacity to escape its pull. He learnt the truth that we human beings need to be saved.

The truth very simply is we cannot save ourselves. When we die, we are completely and totally in the hands of God. We are all sinners, and we cannot presume that we will be admitted to heaven. We cannot demand entrance into heaven. In the end eternal life with God is a gift of God's mercy.

St Paul preaching Christ crucified

One person who understood this well was the Apostle Paul. In the opening chapter of his first letter to the Corinthians, he explains that the power of the Christian message lay not in an attractive human wisdom, but in the power of the message of the cross. He was aware that his preaching must always be about the cross and its power to save.

> For the message of the cross is foolishness to those who are perishing, but to us who are being saved it is the power of God.

This is the great paradox about Christianity. The Gospel the Church proclaims presents the suffering and death of Christ, because it is in this that the power of salvation lies.

Paul speaks about the wisdom of God and the wisdom of the world, and he says wisdom of God seems foolish to the world but for those who grasp this wisdom it is the source of God's saving action in their lives.

> Jews demand signs and Greeks look for wisdom, but we preach Christ crucified: a stumbling block to Jews and foolishness to Gentiles, but to those whom God has called, both Jews and Greeks, Christ the power of God and the wisdom of God. For

> the foolishness of God is wiser than human wisdom, and the weakness of God is stronger than human strength.

Paul understood that the heart of the Christian mystery is the cross of Christ. It is true that many people find this message illogical. The Jews, as he explains, cannot accept it. They are waiting for a Messiah like King David to come back and establish a great kingdom. Having this expectation, the cross makes no sense. Similarly, Paul understands that the Greeks with their great tradition of philosophical thought are looking for deep wisdom. They expect someone with great, exalted ideas and noble aspirations and not somebody whose message is about suffering and dying. The cross makes no sense to them.

Offering his life as a ransom

Throughout the Gospels, Jesus is very conscious that the summation of his life was to be found in his death. The purpose of his coming was really to be found in Calvary. He knew this and he spoke about his impending death many times. He made references to the meaning and significance of his death, even though those closest to him could not grasp what he was saying.

He not only spoke of his death but presented his death as a model of self-sacrifice which should characterise his followers. Thus, he says in Matthew 20:26-28:

> You know that the rulers of the Gentiles lord it over them, and their great men exercise authority over them. It shall not be so

> among you; but whoever would be great among you must be your servant, and whoever would be first among you must be your slave; even as the Son of man came not to be served but to serve, and to give his life as a ransom for many.

Jesus' teaching here is most important. He says that we have to learn to let go of our lives, learn to be servants, learn to be humble. This was the path he took and one that he expects his disciples to embrace. He didn't come to establish himself in power and claim ultimate authority but rather he came to offer his life as a ransom for the salvation of humanity.

In the Gospel of John, chapter 10, we find a similar teaching. Jesus describes himself as the Good Shepherd. The good shepherd, he says, lays down his life for his sheep. Clearly, Jesus is speaking about himself. His life is connected directly to his death. His purpose in coming is all about the cross.

Time and time again this concept is evident in the prophecies of Jesus about his passion and death. Here we are to understand what it really means to be Christian. Christianity is about dying and rising.

Paul, in speaking about baptism, explains that it is a dying with Christ so that one can rise again with him.

> We were therefore buried with him through baptism into death in order that, just as Christ was raised from the dead through the glory of the Father, we too may live a new life

The mystery of Christ's death and resurrection is to be lived out by Christians. In his Letter to the Galatians (2:20) Paul describes how he sees himself,

> I have been crucified with Christ; it is no longer I who live, but Christ who lives in me; and the life that I now live in the flesh I live by faith in the Son of God, who loved me and gave himself for me.

The Christian comes to discover that living a Christian life means a "letting go" of ourselves so that Christ may live in us, and a new life will rise up in us. This is the mystery of Christianity. Although it is hard to grasp and understand, it is a profound truth that Christ saves us, and we can enter into this path of salvation ourselves by dying and rising with him.

This is summarised by the Lord when he teaches in Matthew's Gospel (16:25)

> If any man would come after me, let him deny himself and take up his cross and follow me. For whoever would save his life will lose it, and whoever loses his life for my sake will find it.

This is a challenging profound truth which is difficult for many to grasp and understand and embrace, but Jesus says that if you want to follow him you have to learn to lose your life. Don't hold on to it. If you try to control it, thinking that you can manage your own life because of your own personality, will power and your own capacity, you will lose it. But instead surrender it and let Jesus take over, just as the young man needed to let the lifesaver take over and save him.

That is the way it is with us: learning to let go, learning to surrender and to entrust ourselves to Christ. And Christ will rise up in us and his power will take over and his saving work will be accomplished in us. It is a wonderful, powerful, life-transforming mystery – the beauty and power of Christianity.

Question for personal reflection

Can I remember a time when I experienced losing my life to save it?

8

Jesus is alive

Now we move to the third of the four truths proposed by Pope Francis: "He is alive." This is, in fact, the title of the Apostolic Exhortation that Pope Francis wrote to young people – *Christus Vivit* ("Christ Lives"). This proclamation, central to Christian faith, is our belief that Jesus rose from the dead.

When Pope Francis was talking about this concept to young people, he was making an important point in saying that Jesus is not just a figure of history. We can certainly learn about the life and teaching of Jesus from the Gospels, but Jesus is far more than an historical figure that we can admire and seek to emulate.

Jesus is not just to be seen as someone who is an inspirational figure from the past. His place in our lives involves far more than being a wise and inspiring teacher. He should not be reduced simply to a role model. The Pope is saying there is so much more to Jesus than this. This is because Jesus lives – he has risen from the dead, He is alive!

When we proclaim that Jesus is risen, we are also proclaiming that Jesus continues to engage with his disciples. After he rose from the dead, Jesus appeared to his disciples in his risen glory. He did this firstly to assure his disciples that it was indeed him. This is seen most strikingly in the case of Thomas who doubted that it was really him. He urged Thomas to touch his wounds and put his hand into this pierced side.

When he appeared to his disciples Jesus asked for something to eat, indicating that he was not a ghost or a hallucination. He was not an ephemeral being or an angelic existence but that he was physically risen from the dead. He appeared in a glorified human body.

He wanted the disciples to know that his resurrection was a resurrection of the body. This is what the Church proclaims in the Apostle's creed:

> I believe in the Holy Spirit, the holy Catholic Church, the communion of saints, the forgiveness of sins, the resurrection of the body and life everlasting.

In declaring our faith in the resurrection of Christ from the dead the Creed concludes with the affirmation that we believe in the resurrection of the body and life everlasting. Christ's resurrection is the foretaste of our own sharing in the resurrection of the body and life everlasting.

The Risen Lord engages with us now

One thing worth noting in relation to the appearance of Jesus after the resurrection is who he appeared to. Jesus could have appeared in the temple of Jerusalem or to Pontius Pilate or the high priests to prove his resurrection, but he did not. He appeared to the Twelve and to a broader number of his disciples. In other words, he appeared to those who were believers who would become witnesses of his resurrection.

The story of Jesus accompanying the disciples on the road to Emmaus is one that is rich in meaning for us today. We have already touched on this story but it is worth revisiting the account to note how the risen Lord reveals and engages himself with his close disciples. This is a story for each of us as disciples today.

> That very day two of them were going to a village named Emmaus, about seven miles from Jerusalem, and talking with each other about all these things that had happened. While they were talking and discussing together, Jesus himself drew near and went with them. But their eyes were kept from recognising him. And he said to them, "What is this conversation which you are holding with each other as you walk?"

What is significant about this is not only did Jesus accompany the two disciples, but he engaged with them by asking what they were talking about. He indicated that he was interested in their life and the issues they were discussing. In other words, Jesus is asking: "what is happening in your life, I am interested to know the issues you are contending with".

St Luke (24:18-21), goes on to recount how the disciples were lamenting that the hopes they had had for Jesus of Nazareth were now dashed. They were confused and downcast and uncertain as to what it all meant.

Then they spoke about some women from their group discovering that the tomb was empty and that they claimed to have had a vision of angels who declared that he was alive. In other words, the disciples were saying they couldn't make sense of what has happened. How often do things happen in our life and we cannot make sense of it? We struggle with the meaning, significance or purpose of what has happened and where it is all leading.

St Luke (24:25-27) then records the response of the Lord,

> And he said to them, "O foolish men, and slow of heart to believe all that the prophets have spoken! Was it not necessary that the Christ should suffer these things and enter into his glory?" And beginning with Moses and all the prophets, he interpreted to them in all the Scriptures the things concerning himself.

After Jesus had listened to them and they told him of their confusion, Jesus chooses to enlighten their minds and he reveals the meaning and purpose of his life, death and resurrection to them. Later on, when the disciples reflected back on the conversation the commented (Lk 24:32),

> Did not our hearts burn within us while he talked to us on the road, while he opened to us the Scriptures?

Something was happening to the disciples as Jesus spoke, he was stirring their hearts and he deeply and profoundly touched them by his words. There was a truth, a revelation, that transformed the way the disciples saw things.

This is a wonderful story about the way the risen Lord Jesus wants to engage with us, his disciples today. Firstly, he wants to walk with us on our journey. Secondly, he wants to engage with us about the realities of our life. Jesus wants to reach out to us on our own personal journey. His engagement with us stirs us to open our hearts to him. Jesus, the risen Lord, accompanies each of us on our pilgrimage through life.

Here we might note the final words of St Matthew's Gospel:

> I will be with you always until the end of the age.

These are the parting words that Jesus gives when he commands his disciples to go out into the world proclaiming him to the world. He will be with us until the end of the age. Jesus did not say he was going to be around only on occasions, or in the background of our lives, but he says he will be with us always until the end of the age. This is an extraordinary and beautiful promise of the risen Lord.

We can take a moment to hear these words being spoken to each one of us – "I am going to be with you always". For us, as Christians, we do not just have to go back into history to look for a model or an exemplar of how we should live. We have a living relationship with Jesus because Jesus is alive and he is risen. And he wants to walk with his disciples, just as he did after his resurrection. He manifested himself, appearing to his disciples. They knew that he was alive and that he was with them. Jesus, our risen Saviour, wants us to know the same reality as well. Jesus wants to be with us – this is the wonder of the Resurrection.

As the risen Lord, he can do something that he couldn't do when he was limited by the physical reality of his presence – then he could only be at one place at one time – but as the risen Lord he can be with each one of us individually and personally. He appeared to his disciples, so he wants to appear to us and be with us as his disciples.

Abide in me and I abide in you

In John's Gospel, Chapters 14–17, known as the "Last Supper Discourse", John presents Jesus' final testament to his disciples. Jesus is aware that this was to be the last time he was going to be with his close disciples. He intended to transform the Jewish ritual of the Passover Meal into what we now know as the Sacrament of the Holy Eucharist.

What Jesus did in the Last Supper only really makes sense in light of Calvary and the Resurrection.

At the Last Supper, Jesus was preparing for the next phase of his relationship with his disciples after his death and resurrection. So, the Last Supper was not just a culmination of his time with his disciples, but it was directed to the life of his disciples after his death and after his resurrection. One should read the Last Supper Discourse always thinking about the death and resurrection and the reality of the relationship that his disciples were to have with him as the Risen Lord.

In John, Chapter 15, there is a particular image used by Jesus. It carries through the whole chapter. It is the image of the vine and branches. Again, this image cannot be read except from the perspective of the resurrection. It doesn't really make sense otherwise. Jesus says,

> Remain in me, as I also remain in you. No branch can bear fruit by itself; it must remain in the vine. Neither can you bear fruit unless you remain in me. I am the vine; you are the branches. If you remain in me and I in you, you will bear much fruit; apart from me you can do nothing. If you do not remain in me, you are like a branch that is thrown away and withers; such branches are picked up, thrown into the fire and burned. If you remain in me and my words remain in you, ask whatever you wish, and it will be done for you. This is to my Father's glory, that you bear much fruit, showing yourselves to be my disciples.

These words would not make sense if they referred to a relationship with a physical person but when it pertains to the risen Lord, it makes a lot of sense.

Jesus is saying that he is going to be the principle of life and the principle of fruitfulness in the life of his disciples. He is saying that as the disciple unites him or herself with Jesus, then his risen life will flow into them and that's what will produce a real fruitfulness in their lives. As Christians, we think that we have to live a certain kind of way of life and do the right thing. That is true. But Jesus is saying, "live in me, let me be the source of inspiring the way you live and that is where the real fruitfulness will come".

Jesus is speaking of the new way by which he will be at the heart of the life of each of his disciples. He is saying to his disciples, to us, "Through your relationship with me, my risen life will flow in and through your life and produce real fruitfulness from your life". This only makes sense because of the Resurrection. We are privileged as Christians to have such a relationship with the risen Christ. The more we engage ourselves with Him, the more his life will animate ours.

St Patrick's Breastplate

Men and women of faith have understood that the risen Christ envelops all aspects of their life. Their desire is that he abide in them fully and be the inspiration to all they are and do.

An ancient hymn attributed to St Patrick beautifully captures this and reflects the faith that he brought to Ireland. St Patrick's Breastplate expresses the desire of the believer that Christ will abide in them and that God's protection will always accompany them.

It is envisaged that this prayer be said when one arises in the morning. Saying it we can envisage the risen Lord being the principal of our life.

> Christ with me, Christ before me,
> Christ behind me, Christ in me,
> Christ beneath me, Christ above me,

Christ on my right, Christ on my left,
Christ when I lie down, Christ when I sit down,
Christ when I arise,
Christ in the heart of every man who thinks of me,
Christ in the mouth of every man who speaks of me,
Christ in every eye that sees me,
Christ in every ear that hears me.

Question for personal reflection

How have I sensed that the risen Christ is with me?

9

Empowered by the Spirit

As we have noted, the Last Supper Discourse was oriented to the circumstances of the Apostles after the death and resurrection of the Lord. What is significant is that at the Last Supper Jesus was far more focussed on the fate of his closest disciples than upon his own fate. He was thinking about his mission being continued through the Church.

We cannot listen to those words, without being conscious about what Jesus is doing to prepare his disciples for not only what will immediately follow but also for the new reality of their faith and relationship with him after his death and resurrection. He is really speaking about the time of the Church. Jesus, in speaking to his disciples at the Last Supper, is looking to the reality of things after his death and resurrection. This is the reason for what Jesus did in instituting the Blessed Eucharist.

Pope Francis proposed to young people a fourth truth: "the Spirit gives life". The question of the role of the Holy Spirit in the life of each believer was a very important aspect of the words of Christ at the Last Supper. Three times Jesus spoke of the intention to send the Holy Spirit to his disciples. He is mentioned twice in chapter 14 and once in chapter 16 of John's Gospel.

The promise of the Holy Spirit

We read in John 14:16,

> And I will ask the Father, and he will give you another Counsellor, to be with you forever.

Some bible translations use the word "Advocate" or "Helper" in preference to the word, "Counsellor". Jesus is aware that he was not going to be physically with his disciples in the way that they have known his presence up till this point, but that he had a plan to ask the Father for a special helper for them in the time ahead.

Jesus will not abandon them and leave them to their own resources in continuing his work. Thus, we read in John 14:18,

> I will not leave you desolate.

Jesus is conscious that his disciples will be shocked by what is about to take place through his passion and death on the cross. It will be a great scandal to them. It will shake their faith to the core. They will be confused. While they must endure a period of darkness Jesus intends to ensure their future. He promised that he will not desert them but will give them a gift that will enable them to carry out the mission he entrusts to them. This gift is the gift of the Holy Spirit.

The way that Jesus describes the Holy Spirit in John 14:17 is as a "Spirit of truth." In John 14:26, Jesus says,

> But the Counsellor, the Holy Spirit, whom the Father will send in my name, he will teach you all things, and bring to your remembrance all that I have said to you.

Up until this point, the disciples have been able to receive Jesus' teaching immediately and directly as he spoke to them. They had become used to benefitting from his guidance over the previous three years. Now he would not be able to do this. Jesus said that he would give them someone who would help them continue to hear his voice and receive instruction, teaching and guidance.

In the Sacrament of Confirmation, we speak of the seven gifts of the Holy Spirit. This list of gifts is taken from Isaiah 11; they are the marks of the life and character of the Messiah.

The first three gifts mentioned are wisdom, understanding and knowledge. One of the Holy Spirit's actions is to give wisdom (insight), knowledge and understanding. The Holy Spirit comes to enlighten the mind. In particular these gifts will enable a person of faith to remain true to the faith amidst all the swirl of ideas that can influence the mind.

The more we open our lives to the Holy Spirit, the more we seek the guidance and wisdom of the Holy Spirit, the more we will be sustained in the truth and walk the path marked by God's wisdom and purpose.

The deeper we live a life in the Holy Spirit the more we will receive divine wisdom. We will perceive things the way God perceives them because our mind will be enlightened by divine truth. Rather than relying upon our own native capacity to discern what is right and good, it is God who will reveal the truth to us.

In the world today, this is an important activity of the Holy Spirit. With all the claims and attitudes of the world that flood in on us, one of the great challenges is to be able to live in the truth. God has given the Holy Spirit to enable us to know the way we should go. The more that we allow the Holy Spirit to reveal God's truth to us, the more we will be able to stay in the truth.

In the third reference to the Holy Spirit (John 16:7) we note a very interesting comment by the Lord,

> Nevertheless, I tell you the truth: it is to your advantage that I go away, for if I do not go away, the Counsellor will not come to you, but if I go, I will send him to you.

It's almost as though Jesus is saying what will be coming next is going to be better than what you currently know now. This is an interesting comment. It is saying that we today are not only not disadvantaged by not knowing Jesus in the flesh, but we are better placed to be able to know him and follow him.

Holy Spirit in the Church

In the Acts of the Apostles, which is the story of the birth and early growth of the Church, one sees right from the start that the Holy Spirit is critical to the life of the Church.

In speaking with his Apostles after the Resurrection Jesus outlines what is about to happen. In Acts 1:4 we read,

> And while staying with them he charged them not to depart from Jerusalem, but to wait for the promise of the Father, which he said, "you heard from me, for John baptised with water, but before many days you shall be baptised with the Holy Spirit".

The risen Lord instructs his Apostles that after his Ascension they are to wait in Jerusalem for the promise to be fulfilled - the promise that he spoke about at the Last Supper.

The comparison between the Baptism of John and the Baptism they are about to receive is very important. Jesus explains that John's baptism was a symbolic act of someone wanting to reform their life – it was a baptism of repentance. But the Baptism that Jesus is offering is different. This will be a baptism through the power and presence of the Holy Spirit.

This is important for us in understanding the meaning of our Christian baptism. The sacrament is not just a ritual, less a naming ceremony, but it is a sacramental moment where the power of the Holy Spirit comes upon the baptised.

We read later in the first chapter of Acts of Apostles (1:8),

> But you shall receive power when the Holy Spirit has come upon

you; and you shall be my witnesses in Jerusalem and all of Judea and Samaria and to the end of the earth.

Jesus predicts that something powerful is going to happen to them once the Holy Spirit comes. This is fulfilled at Pentecost. The two signs of the advent of the Holy Spirit at Pentecost are a rush of wind and tongues of fire settling on the heads of each of them.

Acts of the Apostles recounts how this experience was a powerful moment of personal transformation for each of the Apostles. They knew that something significant had occurred to them. The power of the Holy Spirit was real and his presence tangible.

We know the story well: they became witnesses firstly in Jerusalem and ultimately to the ends of the earth. At Pentecost, the disciples were baptised with the Holy Spirit.

The Holy Spirit in the life of the believer

When one reads the New Testament, time and time again there is reference to the Holy Spirit. The Spirit was not just a gift given at Pentecost, the Spirit became an active agent in the life and ministry of the Apostles.

The presence of the Holy Spirit as revealed in the New Testament operates on two levels. The first is the effect of the Holy Spirit in the individual Christian's life. When one reads the New Testament, many times there is reference made to the individual Christians experiencing the Holy Spirit in such a way that there are spiritual manifestations in their life.

The experience of the first Christians is that the presence of the Holy Spirit has real effects in their lives. One expression of this is found in Paul's letter to the Galatians. He speaks of the Holy Spirit being a real and effective sanctifying influence. He describes what he calls the "fruits of the Spirit" (Gal 5:22).

> But the fruit of the Spirit is love, joy, peace, patience, kindness, goodness, faithfulness, gentleness, self-control; against such there is no law.

When one plants a fruit tree, fruits will eventually come forth. For example, apple trees eventually produce apples, similarly with orange trees producing oranges in due time. The fruitfulness is produced from the tree. Having the Holy Spirit within us ensures that the fruits of holiness come forth. It is not so much that we produce the fruit but, as Paul says, if you live your life in the Spirit and allow the Spirit to become the principle of your life, you will find that fruitfulness will come forth, just like they burst forth on the branches of a tree.

The fruits listed by Paul are really the qualities of God himself – love, joy, peace, patience, kindness, goodness, faithfulness, gentleness, self-control. In other words, divine life finds expression in our life not by our own efforts but rather by the work of the Holy Spirit.

We do need to live a virtuous life and do the right thing and develop certain qualities of character and virtues, but, in the end, it is not so much that the fruits have come forth because of our effort, rather it is because God's Spirit produces them in us. We can really try, for example, to be more patient, or try not to get angry, we try hard to do the right thing and live as we should live. We may manage reasonably well. However, if we are really open to the presence of the Spirit, we will find that we will become more patient, anger will just dissipate, and we become more peaceful.

In other words, it is not the result of only our effort, but the fruitfulness is from the work of God's Holy Spirit. In the end, we become holy. Holiness is the work of the Spirit and not just the result of our efforts. Yes, we must make an effort, but we leave the fruitfulness up to God.

Paul says at the end of his letter to the Ephesians (2:10),

> For we are God's handiwork, created in Christ Jesus to do good works, which God prepared in advance for us to do.

This text is sometimes translated as "we are God's work of art". God has created something in us that is beyond that which we can ever imagine ourselves because the Spirit produces these good fruits in us.

The Holy Spirit in the life of the Church

The second dimension of the action of the Holy Spirit is that the Holy Spirit is the agent for the animation of the life and mission of the Church. This is best described in 1 Corinthians

12 where Paul uses the analogy of the human body that is made up of many parts. He uses this image to describe the nature of the Christian community.

In the Christian community the one Spirit is its point of unity. However, this unity is expressed in a diversity of gifts within the community. For example, in a parish there are people that contribute to the life and mission of the parish in a variety of ways. Musicians provide their gift of music. Someone else might have the gift of charity and might want to be involved with St Vincent de Paul for example. Yet others might have the gift of service and are very content to serve without the need for recognition.

Paul says that these different gifts aid the life of the community. People contribute according to their gifts. People have different callings yet Paul reminds us that is all the work of the one Spirit. Different and diverse gifts and ministries all work in harmony for the good of the Church.

Paul understands well that it is the Holy Spirit who is the principle of life in the Church. It is the Spirit that enables the functioning and activity of the Church.

The Christian life in the end is a life in the Spirit. The Christian life is a life of grace. Peter, too, taught about the influence of the Holy Spirit when he said (1 Pet 2:5)

> like living stones be yourselves built into a spiritual house.

God creates the Church as a spiritual house when each of

us allows the Holy Spirit to shape and mould us, both in our individual Christian life and in our communal life as the Church.

Question for personal reflection

Do I see the way in which the Holy Spirit has helped me in my Christian life?

10

Being a disciple

We have explored the four truths that Pope Francis proposed to young people. These truths are foundational to our identity as Catholics. Is there one word that could encapsulate our identity? I suggest that there is, and that the word is used extensively in the Gospels as designating the identity of those who have chosen to follow Jesus. The word is "disciple". The word is used no less than 261 times in the New Testament.

In Jesus' time those who came to believe in him and wanted to place themselves under his guidance were called his disciples. We can say that today those who believe in Jesus and want to live their lives under his direction can also be called his disciples. We, as Catholics, are disciples of Jesus Christ.

The concept of being a disciple has specific meaning in first century Israel. We note that a number of times people referred to Jesus as "rabbi", a word that means "teacher". Scribes and pharisees were also called "rabbi" as people looked to them as spiritual guides. Thus, the word "rabbi" was not reserved just for Jesus himself, but it was a word commonly used in the culture of the day. Jesus happily embraced the word as a description of who he was in relation to those who came into a close relationship with him. If they were disciples then he was a rabbi, or spiritual master.

The word "disciple" speaks firstly about a particular relationship, a master/disciple relationship. When Jesus called disciples, they entered into a close relationship with him. They accepted him as their teacher, their rabbi, their master. We can identify a certain progression: first, there was an encounter with Jesus (like Andrew and his encounter with Jesus), this is followed by a person coming to believe in Jesus, accepting him as the Messiah (in Andrew's case), or Holy One of God (as Peter would later attest), as Lord and Saviour (as the early Christians proclaimed). This then leads to a relationship of trust, an entrusting oneself (and one's salvation) to the Lord. The disciple allows him or herself to be formed by Jesus, with the intention of imitating him, desiring to become more and more like him. The discipleship process is a process of ongoing encounter, of faith and trust, of being formed and so becoming like. This is the path for anyone who wishes to be a disciple of Jesus Christ.

From the very outset of his public ministry Jesus specifically called some individuals to become his disciples. St Matthew records the calling of some fishermen by the Sea of Galilee (4:18-22):

> As Jesus was walking beside the Sea of Galilee, he saw two brothers, Simon called Peter and his brother Andrew. They

were casting a net into the lake, for they were fishermen. "Come, follow me," Jesus said, "and I will send you out to fish for people." At once they left their nets and followed him. Going on from there, he saw two other brothers, James son of Zebedee and his brother John. They were in a boat with their father Zebedee, preparing their nets. Jesus called them, and immediately they left the boat and their father and followed him.

We note the words of Jesus, "Come, follow me". We can note also that Jesus had in mind that these fishermen would not just be followers but would in their turn become "fishers of men". This call to follow is repeated at the very end of St John's Gospel (21:22) when Jesus simply says to Peter what he said at the outset, "follow me" (Jn 21:19). A disciple is encouraged to have a simple focus for their life – the faithful following of their Master, Jesus.

Forming his disciples

The bulk of Jesus' three years of public ministry was preaching to the crowds, visiting villages and towns, and teaching them. But as time went on, Jesus would take his disciples aside for special instruction. Jesus would give a basic message to the crowds, but he would give more specific instructions to his disciples.

When we read the Gospels, we note that Jesus spent increasingly more time with the disciples, taking them aside and preparing them for the mission that he would entrust to them. The disciples were spending more time directly in formation. They were growing in their relationship with him, spending more time with Jesus. Thus, their personal relationship with him increases and no doubt their intimacy with him increases.

At the end of John Chapter 6 after Jesus had given his sublime teaching about being the Bread of Life we are told that many of his disciples could not accept this teaching. We are told that after this many of his disciples drew back and no longer walked with him. Jesus turned to the Twelve and asked them, "Will you also go away?" Simon Peter answered him,

> Lord to whom shall we go? You have the words to eternal life; and we have believed and have come to know that you are the Holy One of God.

Peter here was reflecting what had happened to all the Twelve – in their hearts was an absolute conviction that Jesus was the "Holy One of God". A disciple comes to that place of complete and total faith, trust, confidence and surrender and all they want to be is a faithful disciple.

It might be worth mentioning the fact that while Peter makes his very clear commitment of his own faith in Jesus at this time there would be a moment of fear and anxiety during Jesus's trial where he would deny ever knowing Jesus.

Disciples can fail. Despite everything that they have learnt and the conviction that has grown in them and knowing that Jesus is the one they want to follow and that his teaching is right, but disciples also fail. Jesus knows that Peter loves him, believes in him, and wants to follow him but in a moment of fear and anxiety, he panicked and abandoned his faith. In John, Chapter 21, Jesus will ask Peter three times does he love him. The three affirmations of love counter the three moments of denial.

Disciples go through these struggles where they can lose heart, but they know deep down inside that Jesus is the one they want to follow. Disciples are not perfect. If they wander away for a while, if they fall short or lose faith for a while, that relationship with Jesus has grown to the extent that the disciple will come back. Because there is nowhere else to go, they know that Jesus is the Holy One of God. Disciples reach that point where they know that Jesus is the Way, the Truth and the Life and they come back to rebuild their relationship with him.

Discipleship is a decision

One thing that is important about a disciple is that a disciple has made a decision that is intentional. This is the difference between the crowds and the disciples. The crowds are around and might be inspired by Jesus, they might have found Jesus intriguing, or someone who gives them hope or a purpose to their life. But a disciple is the one that makes a decision. Someone who decides that they want to follow Jesus all their life.

There is a difference in wanting to know Jesus, hearing about him, maybe even wanting to be like him in various ways but still being at "arms length" in the relationship. A disciple is the one who gets closer and closer. The relationship gets stronger and stronger, and the person makes a very clear and definitive decision. "I believe in you; I trust in you, and I give myself completely to you" – that is a disciple.

There are some qualities that identify what makes a disciple, and how a person lives as a disciple.

Firstly, a disciple is one who seeks to learn from the master. It will always be the case that one will want to continue to learn. Being a disciple is a life-long journey. The most basic place for us today to learn from Jesus is through reading Sacred Scripture on a regular basis. A disciple wants to learn and to grow in the ways of God. Listening to the teaching of Sacred Scripture is an important way to continue on the path of learning.

When we go to Mass we are offered this through the Liturgy of the Word. This is a time to be attentive and desire to hear what God may be saying to us. In addition, there is a need to read the Scriptures individually and personally on a daily basis, to take time to be attentive to the Word of God.

A practice known as *Lectio Divina* is a useful way to develop a receptivity of hearing the Scriptures in the heart and not just about reading to understand (or reading with one's mind). This practice allows one to hear the Scriptures in the heart and in the Spirit and not just in the mind. A true disciple is one who wants to hear in their heart what God is revealing to them. A disciple will learn how to read the Scriptures in such a way that the Word of God really speaks to the depths of their being.

It is not so much what one gets out of Scripture but rather learning to be receptive and responsive to hear the Word of God speaking to one deeply and to hear the voice of God. Through this practice, one learns to listen to the voice of God.

Secondly, a disciple develops a life of prayer. Developing a prayer life can take various forms. A disciple will want to take time to be with Jesus. This could take the form of going before the Blessed Sacrament and being with the Lord. It could also be as simple as setting one's alarm fifteen minutes earlier in the morning to allow time to pray and maybe read the Scriptures too. A disciple will pray each day.

In Luke's Gospel, Chapter 11, we are told that Jesus was praying in a certain place, and when he ceased, one of his disciples said to him,

> Lord, teach us to pray, as John taught his disciples.

What is interesting here is that Jesus himself made prayer an integral part of his life. Whenever Jesus had to make a major decision, he would often go up the mountain and spend all night in prayer. The disciples would have seen Jesus often in prayer. The disciples knew that Jesus was a man of prayer. Prayer was integral to Jesus' daily life. It is a reminder too that as disciples, prayer needs to be integral to our life.

As Catholics, an important part of discipleship is the sacramental life – participation in Holy Mass, Holy Communion, Confession - a disciple will see these as very special and important moments of encounter with Christ. We don't just go to Mass, but we participate in the Mass, seeing it as a moment of encounter with Christ. We are there because we want to be with the Lord, listening to the Word of God, commemorating the Lord's Passion, Death and Resurrection in the Eucharistic Prayer and then receiving Holy Communion. To be a disciple we need to have an active sacramental life.

One last point about being a disciple is that we desire to be like Christ, to imitate Christ. St Paul expressed it simply (I Cor 11:1)

> And you should imitate me, just as I imitate Christ

St Paul reveals two things here, firstly he reveals that he seeks to imitate Christ. A disciple should always look to Christ as the exemplar on how to live life. A disciple should look at the qualities in the character of Christ desiring to be like him. Jesus is always the model, the exemplar, and the inspiration for the Christian.

In Paul's comment he encourages the Corinthians to imitate him as he imitates Christ. In seeking to live the Christian life it is helpful to find someone who can be a model or an example, modelling the Christian life. Perhaps, this person might have developed a particular virtue that can instil inspiration that we can strive to imitate.

One particular application of this is the Catholic tradition of having a spiritual director. Another option is having a particular confessor that helps and supports us in the development of our Christian life.

Another option is to belong to a Christian group that offers teachings in the Christian life. We all need ongoing formation so that we can mature in our Christian way of life.

As Catholics there are the multitude of Saints who are great examples and sources of inspiration. Thus, we seek out those whom we can seek to imitate as they have imitated Christ.

Question for personal reflection

What steps can I take to be a more faithful disciple?

Module 3
Hands: Witnessing to Jesus

11

Becoming missionary disciples

In his first Encyclical Pope Francis addressed the need for the Church to have an evangelising heart. In *Evangelii Gaudium*, (The Joy of the Gospel), he said (EG 120),

> Every Christian is a missionary to the extent that he or she has encountered the love of God in Christ Jesus: we no longer say that we are "disciples" and "missionaries", but rather that we are always "missionary disciples."

Many times, over his pontificate has he returned to this theme. Indeed, in an open letter to the Church in Germany (29 June, 2019) as they were advancing their approach to synodality he stated,

> True transformation responds to needs arising from our life of faith and from the evangelizing dynamic of the Church. It requires pastoral conversion. We need an attitude that, by trying to live and reveal the Gospel, breaks with "the grey pragmatism of the daily life of the Church, in which all appears to proceed normally, while in reality faith is wearing down and degenerating into small-mindedness". Pastoral conversion reminds us that evangelisation must be our guiding criterion par excellence, on the basis of which we discern all the steps we are called to take as an ecclesial community. Evangelisation is the essential mission of the Church.

Pope Francis is in no doubt that the key to a true transformation of the Church is embracing the "evangelising dynamic".

So far in our reflections we have explored the transformation of the heart that occurs when a person truly encounters Jesus Christ. In the second Module we examined our identity as Christians. This third Module under the image of "Hands" will consider the way in which we can be witnesses to Jesus Christ.

Pope Francis offers us an important insight. We cannot be satisfied with only being disciples. A disciple is someone who sits at the master's feet, someone who learns and is under the guidance of the master, who is receptive and wants to be formed. These qualities are all very necessary and one will always be a disciple of Jesus. However, the Pope calls on us to see that something more is required of us. We must not only be disciples but must become "missionary disciples".

How to be missionary

The question now is how can we, as Catholics, be missionary? Often the immediate reaction to this proposal is that such an idea is a daunting one. Most people are happy to meet the Lord, even happy to be a disciple but being a missionary is something that is seen as very challenging, especially for Catholics. So, we need to consider how we can be missionary and to realise that being a missionary disciple is not that difficult and impossible to do.

As Catholics, there is a tendency for us to want to keep our faith private. We get easily embarrassed when we have to talk about our faith and "wear our heart on our sleeve". We prefer to live our faith privately.

While this is easily understandable, the Lord wants more from each person than that. We cannot just settle into quiet anonymity, avoiding potential awkwardness or worse if we declare what we believe.

It has been my experience when I have been involved with someone wanting to become a Catholic by going through RCIA (Rite of Christian Initiation of Adults), to discover that the person has been thinking about it for years but did not take the step.

I have encountered many individuals who have told me that they wanted to become a Catholic for a long time. When I asked them why they were so slow to respond, the person said "Well, no one ever asked me".

There are people who are open to being involved in the life of the Church, wanting to know more about God and wanting to become a Catholic but the reason they haven't done it is because no one has ever asked them.

This sometimes happens when one spouse is not a Catholic but comes along to Mass with the family and helps raise the children and gets quite involved, but nobody ever asked them the question: "do you want to become a Catholic?".

We Catholics should examine our consciences. Have we inadvertently held someone back from embracing the faith because we have been too reluctant to actually speak to them about the faith and invite them to join the Church?

Let us consider an example of someone who invited his friend to meet the Lord. It follows the account of Andrew encouraging his brother, Simon, to meet Jesus whom he was convinced was the Messiah. John the Evangelist then follows with this story,

> The next day Jesus decided to leave for Galilee. Finding Philip, he said to him, "Follow me." Philip, like Andrew and Peter, was from the town of Bethsaida. Philip found Nathanael and told him, "We have found the one Moses wrote about in the Law, and about whom the prophets also wrote—Jesus of Nazareth, the son of Joseph." "Nazareth! Can anything good come from there?" Nathanael asked. "Come and see," said Philip.

Note the simple invitation that Phillip made to his friend, Nathaniel, "come and see". Philip didn't attempt to give his friend a long explanation of why he came to believe in Jesus. He didn't give a great theological explanation about the Messiah, who He is going to be or what He is going to do or go into great detail or get into lengthy argument to explain things fully.

Often, we baulk about speaking about our faith because we can feel inadequate in explaining ourselves. Philip just issued a simple invitation. We don't need to have the theological expertise, to know how to answer the difficult questions.

This is, in fact, similar to what Andrew did for his brother, Simon. It was an invitation to the experience of meeting Jesus. When we want to invite someone to something we may be tempted to have to give a full explanation but this is not necessary. There is no need to present things in a way so they can understand, as though it's all going to depend on our arguments or the way we explain things. It can be as simple as, "come and see".

The invitation can begin a process. John goes on to describe the conversation between Jesus and Nathaniel. Nathaniel comes to believe not because Philip has convinced him, but because he has had his own experience of meeting Jesus. Nathanael, also known as Bartholomew, subsequently became a disciple, named as an Apostle, became a missionary and ultimately a martyr.

The word "martyr" is a Greek word which means "witness" – the ultimate witness to Christ is being prepared to die for Christ.

While martyrdom is not an absolute essential part of the process, the other parts are. There is a simple process: from the "come and see" there is an encounter with Christ, faith results, discipleship is embraced and then the person becomes a missionary. This is the process that should happen in every Christian's life.

However, the process all depends on the very first phase, the phase of being invited to come and experience Christ.

This is the role that Catholics need to play, to provide the opportunity for a person to meet Christ - and then allow Christ will take over. Just like John the Baptist said, "He must increase, and I must decrease." Once we bring someone to Christ, we step back and let Christ then lead the person forward into the ways of faith.

Inviting someone

How can we develop a way of inviting someone?

The first way is by taking opportunities in everyday conversations that we have with people. This can be a simple process. By having a casual conversation about one's life for example, it could be quite natural to mention that we went to Mass on the weekend or participated in some Catholic event. It is important not to push anything or to try and make a point or make oneself appear holier than anyone else but to just be natural – this is who I am.

It is important not to back away from a question or a curiosity that people might have about one's life and one's beliefs. Just allow the conversation to go forward. There is no need to launch into a great explanation about Catholicism. We just allow the conversation to be open, allowing it to go where it will.

One thing that is important to note is that there are many people in society who are searching. They may have drifted away from faith, and there is a void, an emptiness, in their life. They sense that something is lacking.

These days we hear of people referring to themselves as spiritual but not religious. In a way, it is a bit of a cop out. But the other side to this self-understanding is that they do believe that there is something more, a deeper meaning to life, something beyond what is material and obvious, so that is still an opening and a possibility for them to be presented with the possibility of faith.

We should not presume that people are not interested in religion or things of faith because they are, because everyone has a soul and a spiritual dimension to their existence. When people are not living a life of faith, there is something incomplete in their life. So, we can presume that people may open to the questions about God and a spiritual way of life.

We should not presume that they will reject what we say or be dismissive, although, of course, this may happen. But there will be others who will be open to receive and listen to what we may share about our faith.

One of the things that is helpful to consider when we have a conversation with someone on matters of faith is that we have entered into a relationship with the other person. The person knows something that is important to us and we know that the other person is searching.

It is important not to make the one conversation the beginning and the end and the only opportunity to share. It doesn't have to be the one sole conversation that achieves a result. In this regard Pope Francis offers a good insight when he speaks about the idea of accompanying people, of "walking" with them. This idea of being able to walk with a person over a period of time and so build a relationship allows for further conversations to take place. Coming to faith is most often a journey. So, we allow it to happen incrementally and sometimes this might take years.

Not ashamed of the Gospel

It is possible that sometimes we open up about our faith and there is a reaction which causes us embarrassment. It is important not to allow those times of rejection to lead to the point of discouragement. We can be tempted to think that it is all too hard, it doesn't work, and so we back away from doing it.

It is worth hearing these words from St Paul found in Romans 1:16:

> For I am not ashamed of the gospel: it is the power of God for salvation to everyone who has faith.

It is important that if there is a set-back, not to back away completely, but to wait for another opportunity and to persist and not give up.

Pope St John Paul II expressed it well when he said that, as

Christians, we should "propose but not impose". In other words, we present the faith to people as a recommendation but we never force the issue.

We Catholics are averse to heavy handed tactics or trying to force someone by sheer determined argument, but at the same time this does not mean that we should not endeavour to lead people to faith. It is useful to understand that we do not impose but rather we wish to propose something that is so important to us and may be a source of new life for the person we are sharing with. Thus, there is a gentle but firm persistence in our approach.

In effect what we are saying is: "I have got something to offer, something that is important to me that I want to share with you that gives life and joy to me". We make an offer to a person and the person is free to accept it or not.

Another helpful way to approach offering an invitation is to use the image of traffic lights – red, yellow and green. If we feel that there is much resistance and the possibility of an argument is coming, that signifies a red light, so we should stop. No need to push it if we feel that it is a red light. A yellow light, on the other hand, occurs when one is speaking to someone who is not quite on the same page, but they are not disinterested either, this indicates a yellow light and accordingly, we should slow down, and not say too much. Drawing on our road experience when we are stopped and the yellow light comes on, we start off slowly. Thus, we may resume our conversation gently. The green light is a go and provides a chance to take it forward – in other words, we can offer the invitation, "come and see".

Inviting to what?

If we would like to invite someone, what should we be inviting them to? Inviting someone to Mass might be sometimes possible but it also might be a bridge too far. We could be throwing someone in the deep end. It may be far wiser to initially seek to build the relationship. We could invite someone for a cup of coffee or, if the relationship has developed sufficiently, we could invite them to our home. When someone invited comes into our home, they are being invited into a Christian home. Christian images are in evidence. They have a chance to see that there is something special and different about this family. It gives them an insight into the values that the family lives by. We should not underestimate the impact that Catholic family life can have on people who have not known what it means to be a family inspired by the Christian faith.

Another example is inviting someone to a Christian event. There might be something happening in our parish. There they experience the atmosphere of a Christian community. In other situations, we can consider inviting a person to a rosary or Adoration.

When the Palavra Viva community from Brazil were in Tasmania, they used to have 10–15 university students for Sunday lunch and then take them to the chapel for a time of prayer. They would expose the Blessed Sacrament, have a time of Adoration. One student, who was Hindu, started to ask questions after Adoration and although it was something new to her, she felt something that touched her during this time of prayer. This eventually led her to asking to become a Catholic.

In the gospels, as we have noted, Jesus was often at people's places for meals. The story of Zacchaeus wherein Jesus invited himself is an example. Jesus would often be at the houses of unbelievers like the tax collectors and sinners and was often criticised for this. However, he did it to reach out to them and to engage with them to invite them into faith. Jesus sets an example for us. It is important to see that this is not something that is too challenging. If we have a heart to draw people to know Christ then we can find ways to reach out to them and offer some invitation that may well set them on a path to the faith.

Question for personal reflection

Could you compose a list of four or five people whom you would like to reach out to?

12

Witnessing to our faith

Being a missionary disciple can begin simply with an intention to reach out to people and invite them to "come and see". Let us see how we can take our missionary task one simple step further. The next step in drawing people closer to Christ is to give a simple witness to our faith.

Witnessing is different to preaching. In witnessing we are not presenting the arguments for faith in Christ nor does it involve presenting a theological explanation of the faith. Rather the essence of witness is a simple sharing of what God has done in our life.

Pope Francis, in speaking about becoming missionary disciples, said

> Every Christian is a missionary to the extent that he or she has encountered the love of God in Christ Jesus.

What we have to share with others is what we have encountered – our experience of the love of God in Jesus Christ. When a person experiences love, they just have to share with others. The Christian has known the love of God in Christ and simply wants to share this with others.

When we witness to the faith we are talking about our experience of God's love for us, how He has touched our lives, how He has revealed Himself to us and how He has moved in our life in a way that has changed us and has enriched us. It is our story. Its authenticity lies in the fact that we are able to share what has happened to us.

Witnessing our faith is about witnessing to the love of God. Just as someone in love cannot hold back from its wonderful effect in their life, they can't but share what has happened to them. It is written all over them and they can't help but want to share their experience of love with others. That is what Pope Francis is saying: because one has encountered the love of God in Christ Jesus, one becomes a missionary disciple, wanting to share the experience of Jesus.

After his Resurrection the Risen Lord called on his disciples to become witnesses to him "to the end of the earth" (Acts 1:8).

> But you shall receive power when the Holy Spirit has come upon you; and you shall be my witnesses in Jerusalem and in all Judea and Samaria and to the end of the earth.

This is what Jesus expects of us. Early in the Gospels he said that his disciples are to be salt to the earth and light to the world. We are not to hide our light under a bushel basket. We cannot be anonymous as Christians. Let us hear this admonition again (for we have heard it many times). Now, considering being missionary disciples we can let the Lord's words penetrate our minds and hearts.

> You are the salt of the earth. But if the salt loses its saltiness, how can it be made salty again? It is no longer good for anything, except to be thrown out and trampled underfoot. You are the light of the world. A town built on a hill cannot be hidden. Neither do people light a lamp and put it under a bowl. Instead they put it on its stand, and it gives light to everyone in the house. In the same way, let your light shine before others, that they may see your good deeds and glorify your Father in heaven.

We are called to be salt and light. To let our light shine.

Witness

The word "witness" means someone who reports on what has happened. When there is a car accident we hear the news report speaking of witnesses to the event. In a court of law a witness is asked to present faithfully and truly what they saw happen. Thus, being a witness is simply about telling one's story and one's experience. The first thing about being a witness is being faithful to oneself and one's personal experience.

In the Acts of the Apostles, as well as the account of the conversion of Paul on the road to Damascus, Luke records Paul giving his witness to what happened to him. We could imagine that Paul often told the story of his conversion. Thus, we read in Acts Chapter 22 that Paul has returned to Jerusalem and he is given an opportunity to speak before the council of the Jews. He begins by saying,

> I am a Jew, born at Tarsus in Cilicia, but brought up in this city at the feet of Gamaliel, educated according to the strict manner of the law of our fathers, being zealous for God as you all are this day. I persecuted this Way to the death, binding and delivering to prison both men and women, as the high priest and the whole council of elders bear me witness.

Note what Paul does - he begins his witness by talking about his life prior to his moment of conversion. The people would have seen Paul as a bold Christian preacher and might have thought that he was always like that. But by relating how he was before, he showed the people that he was just like them.

Reading on further in Acts 22:6 Paul recounts his conversion moment:

> As I made my journey and drew near to Damascus, about noon a great light from heaven suddenly shone about me. And I fell to the ground and heard a voice saying to me, "Saul, Saul, why do you persecute me?" And I answered, "Who are you, Lord?" And he said to me, "I am Jesus of Nazareth whom you are persecuting."

In this passage, Paul is telling succinctly and clearly what happened to him on the road to Damascus. He explained his profound personal experience of being struck down and hearing the Lord speak to him.

When we look over his many letters in the New Testament, there is a sense that time and time again Paul wants to share the transformation that took place in his life because of this encounter on the road to Damascus. He did not just present arguments for the validity of his message, he wanted to share that happened to him personally. He knew that by talking about his personal account of his conversion, he was able to explain why he had the kind of faith that he had.

Thus, in giving our witness we are saying, "I was living a particular way, living in the world engaged with all sorts of things that would seem to be normal to most people. But then there was a moment of encounter, a moment of grace, a moment of enlightenment, a moment in which I felt the presence of God touch my life, change my life, and that has led me to the faith I have today."

Some people might be able to give that kind of testimony. The story of personal conversion is a very powerful one because when a person shares the first part of their life story, they are in a way relating to people who can identify with what is being said. But then when they hear of the conversion, then those listening to the story can also realise that they too can change. They realise that God can also act in their life in the way He acted in the life of the person giving the testimony.

Some testimonies may be sudden and dramatic as in Paul's case, but for others it might be gradual and something that has happened slowly over time. Others might have grown up in the faith so there was no particular moment of conversion from one way of life to a new way of life as a Christian. However, all of us who are now living a life of faith can identify ways in which God has intervened in our life. This is our story and a story we can share. We can all share something of the way that God has moved in our lives.

Wonderful works of God

In the Psalms there are references to psalmists wanting to give witness to what God has done for them. They want to share the "wonderful works of God".

Thus, for example, in Psalm 22:22 we read,

> I will tell of your name to my brethren; in the midst of the congregation I will praise you.

Similarly, in Psalm 66: 16, we read,

> Come and hear, all you who fear God, and I will tell what he has done for me.

Being a witness in the end is nothing more than wanting to tell what God has done in our life.

There is probably no better expression of the desire to share what God has done than in the great hymn of Mary, the Magnificat. It is a beautiful joy-filled expression of wonder at what God has done for her.

> My soul proclaims the greatness of the Lord. My spirit rejoices in God my Saviour. Because the Almighty has done great things for me, holy is His name.

When we give our witness, we desire to give glory to God. While the witness is about a person's own experience, it is not really about the person, but rather about what God has done.

We do not want to direct the attention to us. It is not about us. Thus, when giving our witness we can test what we are saying by asking: Is God receiving all the glory. The Virgin Mary is our model:

> The Almighty has done great things for me holy is his name.

Thus, we can pause and ask ourselves – what can I give witness to? We all have a story, and each one is unique.

"Tell no one"

One of the curious things we can see in the Gospels is that sometimes when Jesus would heal a person, he would ask them not to tell anyone. While that seems strange, we can possibly understand why Jesus did this. He was worried that people might treat him as a wonder worker and would be so caught up with the miracles that they would not hear his message. At times, when people got so excited, he would need to calm the crowd down, as we see in the case of the feeding of the five thousand. Jesus sent the people away and went up into the hills.

When Jesus asked people not to publicise what he had done for them, it was so that the attention was not to be directed towards him. He did not want to become a celebrity, a miracle worker. Thus, we, too, want to avoid having attention directed towards us.

However, on other occasions, he encouraged people to share

their experience. This was the case in the story of the demoniac when Jesus drove out the demon. We read in St Luke's Gospel, 8:38–39,

> The man from whom the demons had gone begged that he might be with him; but he sent him away, saying, "Return to your home, and declare how much God has done for you." And he went away, proclaiming throughout the whole city how much Jesus had done for him.

In this instance Jesus wanted him to share with the people what God had done for him. And this is what the Lord asks of us too, to share what God has done for us.

Another story is the one from John's Gospel when Jesus healed the blind man in the temple on the Sabbath day causing a lot of controversy (Jn 9:24-25). When challenged by the Pharisees the blind man boldly declares what has happened to him,

> A second time they summoned the man who had been blind. "Give glory to God by telling the truth," they said. "We know this man is a sinner." He replied, "Whether he is a sinner or not, I don't know. One thing I do know. I was blind but now I see!"

To give witness is simply to share what we know has happened to us. Every witness will be individual and particular. It is not important whether it is great and powerful or if it is simple, but it is important because you know what God has done for you. You know how God has acted in your life.

When we look at our own witness, we should dismiss the idea that I don't have anything worthwhile to say. Sometimes it can be the very simple things that you are able to share that do have an impact on others. And there can be occasions where we have a simple story from our life that just might be the most appropriate thing at that moment. So, don't think that if it is not dramatic, it is not good. It can be very, very simple.

Giving our witness

Giving our witness is always, in the end, giving glory to God who has done great things in us. In offering our witness we want to capture how God has, in one way or another, changed us for the better. This can sometimes be best expressed by describing an aspect of our life that has changed.

Whenever we offer our witness to others it is always done from a place of humility, and it never seeks to impress or draw attention to ourselves.

When we give our witness we are simply recounting our own experience. It is preferable not to end by giving an exhortation or falling into preaching. We want to let the authenticity of our witness stand in its own right.

However, there can be occasions when it is natural to offer some form of encouragement along the lines that if this can happen to me then it can also happen to you. Our witness can be followed up by a recommendation to do something practical. This can show a person how they can respond to what they have heard.

In the heart of a missionary disciple is a desire to give glory to God by recounting the wonderful things He has done for us.

Question for personal reflection

Can you recall when someone shared their testimony

and how it affected you?

13

How to give your testimony

While we have spoken about witnessing to our faith, it is still a daunting task for many Catholics. We feel uncomfortable about speaking of our personal faith. We fear rejection or social isolation. It can also be the case that we doubt we have any significant spiritual experience that has relevance to others.

In this chapter we will explore further the question of giving witness to our faith.

St Peter encouraged the first Christians to be ready to offer a witness to their faith (I Pet 3:15-16):

> But in your hearts revere Christ as Lord. Always be prepared to give an answer to everyone who asks you to give the reason for the hope that you have. But do this with gentleness and respect, keeping a clear conscience, so that those who speak maliciously against your good behaviour in Christ may be ashamed of their slander.

A natural starting point to explore what we may have to offer is to reflect on how our faith in Christ has changed and shaped our lives. John had no doubt that his experience of Christ radically changed his life (I Jn 1:1-4).

> That which was from the beginning, which we have heard, which we have seen with our eyes, which we have looked upon and touched with our hands, concerning the word of life - the life was made manifest, and we saw it, and testify to it, and proclaim to you the eternal life which was with the Father and was made manifest to us – that which we have seen and heard we proclaim also to you, so that you may have fellowship with us; and our fellowship is with the Father and with his Son Jesus Christ. And we are writing this that our joy may be complete.

John is giving clear testimony to the fact that he knows his life has been radically changed and he rejoices in what has happened to him and he longs for others to share in what he has experienced. John knows that he is now in real and effective union with God. He knows that he is on the path to eternal life in heaven.

There is an evident joy and excitement as he shares what his faith means to him. This is the spirit that each of us need: we know what encountering Christ has meant for us and we want others to share in this experience.

People who do not know Christ can be searching in various ways. They may be at a point when they simply need someone to lead them to the next step in their faith. For most people the path to conversion is a slow and steady one. One step is taken, a time may elapse, then something leads the person to take another step. St Paul comments that one person sows, another waters (see I Cor 3:8). In other words, the path to conversion may be assisted by different people at different times. For our part we might just be the right person at the right time.

Consider the story of the encounter between Phillip and the Ethiopian eunuch (Acts 8:26-32)

> But an angel of the Lord said to Philip, "Rise and go...." And he rose and went. And behold, an Ethiopian, a eunuch, ... had come to Jerusalem to worship and was returning; seated in his chariot, he was reading the prophet Isaiah. And the Spirit said to Philip, "Go up and join this chariot." So Philip ran to him, and heard him reading Isaiah the prophet, and asked, "Do you understand what you are reading?" And he said, "How can I, unless someone guides me?" And he invited Philip to come up and sit with him.... And the eunuch said to Philip, "About whom, pray, does the prophet say this, about himself or about someone else?" Then Philip opened his mouth, and beginning with this scripture he told him the good news of Jesus. And as they went along the road they came to some water, and the eunuch said, "See, here is water! What is to prevent my being baptised?" And he commanded the chariot to stop, and they both went down into the water, Philip and the eunuch, and he baptised him. And when they came up out of the water, the Spirit of the Lord caught up Philip; and the eunuch saw him no more, and went on his way rejoicing.

In this passage we can note a couple of things. Firstly, Phillip is prompted by the Holy Spirit. After all, God is the great evangelizer, we are simply his instruments. We may find ourselves spiritually moved to do something that is unexpected – it may be the Holy Spirit urging us.

The eunuch has questions. There are things he does not understand. Phillip explains things simply. When moments come and we are invited to answer a question, don't dismiss the opportunity under the false sense of our own inadequacy. Speak from the heart, from what you understand. It does not need to be "high" theology.

In this instance, the eunuch is already quite advanced on the road to faith and just needs help in moving forward. Philip actually enables him to want to be baptized.

I recall an incident when I was a seminarian. I was hitch-hiking across the Nullarbor Plains and was picked up. When the driver learned that I was a seminarian he began asking all sorts of questions about the faith. I answered as best as I could. The questions became more pointed and I continued to answer them. Suddenly, the driver put his foot on the brakes and stopped the car. He said to me that he wanted to be baptised. Unlike the story of the Phillip and the eunuch we were in the middle of the desert and there was no water! I encouraged him make contact with a priest when he reached his destination.

As we saw before, the Apostle Peter (I Pet 3:15) said,

> Always be prepared to give an answer to everyone who asks you to give the reason for the hope that you have.

We need to be ready to respond to special moments that may come our way. Often, they can be unexpected. But we need to be ready. Perhaps we can recall a moment when we were prompted to share our faith, but we hesitated – it felt awkward, we felt unsure of what to say. Afterwards we may have felt that we missed an opportunity. We sensed that it was a prompting from the Holy Spirit and we failed to step out in faith. Giving witness to our faith does take trust in God and does require a degree of courage.

Preparing your testimony

In order to be ready to "give the reason for the hope that you have", we need to prepare our testimony. Indeed, we can have several testimonies, not just one. If we take time to reflect we can think of different experiences that may be good to share.

The first place to start is to consider the testimony of how God has led you to have the faith you have. You may be able to identify special moments of grace.

You may also have other testimonies – of a healing, of a prayer answered, of a help in your marriage, of a calling to some special work. It is good to have several testimonies in mind as different circumstances can lead to the need for different testimonies.

It is also good to have thought how you can give a two-minute testimony or a twelve-minute testimony, as circumstances will require either a short or a longer testimony.

If we have never done this before there is value in writing your testimony down so that you have rehearsed what you could say.

Some useful points

Whether you have discovered the faith for the first time, or come back to the faith after drifting away, or you have lived your faith steadily, all of us have a personal testimony to offer to others. We can all reflect upon our lives and see what God has done in us. This is what we have to share with others.

When about to prepare your testimony seek the guidance of the Holy Spirit. After all, the Holy Spirit is the real evangeliser. We are simply his instruments.

When you are sharing your testimony engage directly with the person you are speaking with. It is good to establish eye contact and ensure that you are speaking directly to them. It is not a speech that you are delivering but something from the heart. It is your story.

It is important to be able to share your testimony in your own personal way, using words that you are comfortable with. Always keep it humble and simple. People can relate to a real experience and are interested to hear what our experiences are, especially when they mean so much to us.

Always focus on God, and his work in your life. There is no need to give too much detail on what you were like before your conversion, unless you think it may help. We don't want to glorify our sins; rather, the aim is to give all glory to God.

When you share your testimony it is good that you are able to express your genuine gratitude for what God has done in your life. A grateful person is a humble person.

There is no need to provide a lengthy biography of your life. Keep your testimony focussed on its central point.

Be conscious that the person you are speaking with may not be familiar with Catholic terminology. Use common terms rather than technical terms. Be mindful that when giving your testimony, you are also witnessing to the Christian way of life – we must love one another – so always avoid speaking negatively about other people or religious organisations.

It is beneficial to sit down and write out your testimony. This helps to clarify what you can share. It is good to reflect quietly and see how God has moved in your life. We can all discover the movements of God that have shaped us. It is also good to consider how you responded to the grace of God and to consider what it has meant for you. For example, have you found a new joy, peace, or hope?

It is also worth considering what your life in the Church means to you. This is because authentic conversion to Christ includes entry into and participation in his Body, which is the Church. It is also through the Church that we come to encounter the risen Christ. It may be that in the Church you have experienced healing or encouragement to lead a better life. Discovering the fullness of Christian teaching may have brought new clarity to your life.

When you take the time to sit down and write out your

testimony you will find yourself being more aware that God has blessed you, helped you and guided you. Preparing your testimony can actually be a source of renewed appreciation of the love of God for you personally.

Question for personal reflection

Can I now sit down and write out my testimony?

14

Praying with a person

There is another step that we can take in assisting a person to open their hearts and lives to Jesus Christ. It is, in fact, a very powerful step that can have significant results. It is offering to pray with a person.

Again, for many Catholics, this may seem a step too far. But let us see how it can, in fact, be a most loving and beautiful act on our part, and a special moment of grace for the recipient.

In the Gospels, we see that during Jesus' public ministry many people approached him and asked him to help them in their needs or the needs of others. They knew that Jesus was a Rabbi, a teacher, a holy man, a prophet. They believed that he could bring the presence, power, mercy, and the love of God into their lives. As Jesus' reputation spread, more and more people came to Him for healing and asked him to intervene for their needs.

When we read the Gospels, we note that when Jesus was asked to heal someone, he did it right there, on the spot, immediately. He didn't put it off. He didn't say that he will remember the person when he goes to the synagogue on the Sabbath, rather he responded at that moment.

For most of us, when someone asks us to pray for them we say something like, "I will remember you in my prayers", or "I will pray for you at Mass". We are often reluctant to respond immediately and pray with the person.

Let us consider one example, the account of the healing of the servant of the centurion (Mt 8:5-9).

> As he entered Capernaum, a centurion came forward to him, begging him and saying, "Lord, my servant is lying paralysed at home, in terrible distress." And he said to him, "I will come and heal him." But the centurion answered him, "Lord I am not worthy to have you come under my roof; but only say the word, and my servant will be healed. For I am a man under authority, with soldiers under me; and I say to one, "
>
> "Go", and he goes and to another, "Come", and he comes, and to my slave, "Do this", and he does it.

This centurion, being a Roman soldier, was presumably a non-believer, not a member of the Jewish people. However, he was distressed about his servant who may have been a quite integral to his family's life. He was concerned that his servant was seriously ill. He approached Jesus asking for help. Jesus' immediate response is to go to the centurion's house.

The response of the centurion is quite extraordinary. He believes that Jesus can just say the word and his servant will be healed. Such faith!

In a similar story Jesus is asked to heal the daughter of Jairus, a synagogue official. Again, Jesus offers to go immediately to Jairus' house to heal her. Upon their arrival, his daughter was already dead. Jesus does not hesitate but goes in and raises her back to life (see Lk 8:40-42, 49-56).

In another story, one that we have referred to before, we can note something important. In the healing of the leper St Matthew tell us,

> A leper came to him and knelt before him, saying Lord, if you will, you can make me clean." And he stretched out his hand and touched him, saying, "I will; be clean." And immediately his leprosy was cleansed.

In this case, notice that Jesus touches the leper, something that wasn't done during those times as that would render one unclean. However, by touching the leper he creates a personal link with the person. In praying with someone it can be appropriate to place one's hand on the shoulder of the person being prayed with.

Thus, we can sum up. Jesus responds immediately to a request that is made to him. This is important because in the moment the person makes the request there is a moment of grace. The person is open. They have expressed their deep need. In that moment, the person has asked for help. It is important not to let the moment pass. Jesus often said following a healing, "your faith has saved you". The person made an act of faith in approaching him. He responded to their moment of openness.

There is of course an obvious difference between these accounts of miracles in the Gospels and our own situation. Simply, Jesus can do all these healings because Jesus is Jesus, the Son of God, who has the power to do these healings. But for us this is clearly not the same. There is big difference in what Jesus does and what we can do. However, we do not rely upon our own power, the power belongs to Jesus. We are the means by which Jesus can act.

There is a huge difference between Jesus and us. But what we do is call upon his power. We are not the healers. We don't have the capacity to heal. But we have the faith to invoke the healing power of Jesus in a particular situation, for a particular person. We act in faith, trusting in God. So, we pray for people not because we think we have the power, because we don't. But we do it because we know that Jesus has the power to act. We act in faith and leave whatever may happen to the Lord.

Why do people ask us to pray for them? Firstly, it is because people see us as people of faith. The people asking for prayers think that as people of faith we have the capacity to engage the power of God in a situation. We can be quite humbled by this. But the person is in need and we should have the willingness to respond, even if we feel completely inadequate.

It may be the case that the person asking for prayers feels that they are not capable of doing it themselves. Perhaps because they might feel that they don't know how, or perhaps they believe that their faith is not strong enough. They could well be Catholic but perhaps they don't go to Mass, maybe they are far away from God and maybe they may not have God in their life at all, but they have a great personal need. They may look upon someone with faith as more capable of being able to pray because they recognise that a person with faith has a relationship with God.

People ask us to pray for them because they recognise our faith and because they feel we can do a better job than they can. They sense in a person of faith that they have someone who can fill that gap that they feel in their own life. It can be very humbling, and we can feel very inadequate ourselves, but they look to us to do what they perhaps feel that they cannot do.

What we have to do is overcome our own sense of inadequacy or our own sense that it's too much for us to do. It does require a step in our faith. So, in this moment we are being asked to step out in faith. When a person asks us to pray for them, they are actually in a very special position themselves, as they feel their need, they feel they can't deal with the situation in their life, and they need God, and they are turning to God.

They are turning to God through us because they know we are someone who knows God. We are someone who is in relationship with God. This is a moment of grace for both. It is a moment of opportunity when we can be the means by which God acts in their life.

An experience in Rome

I recently led a pilgrimage to Rome with the Catholic Educators from the Archdiocese. After an audience with Pope Francis in St Peter's Square, where there was a crowd of approximately 50,000 people, I planned to meet up with the leaders at a certain place near the colonnades. I was dressed as a bishop in my soutane with its red piping. As the rest of the group were amongst the crowd, it took a while for them to meet up with me. I soon found myself surrounded by many people who approached me seeking a blessing. I must have given at least a hundred blessings to people from different parts of the world and the crowd just kept coming.

I was struck by the humility of the people who came forward to ask for a blessing. Many of them asked for a specific blessing. In one case a young woman in her late twenties from South Carolina, United States, who had with her a small urn of her father's ashes. She asked me to pray for her father. I prayed for her and her father, and tears began to fall from her eyes. This was a moment of grace for her.

I recall another incident. In one of my parishes I was a hospital chaplain. Every Thursday I would go to the hospital and visit all the Catholics in the hospital. As part of this visit, I would ask the patient if they would like to receive Holy Communion, with the intention of returning on the weekend.

There was a particular man that I visited and when I asked if he wanted to receive Holy Communion, he refused, "no thanks

Father". He was still in hospital the following week and I received the same response.

On the third week, I asked him if he would like to receive a blessing instead. The man agreed. I laid my hand on his shoulder and started to pray for him. At this moment the man just broke down, tears running down his face. There was a breakthrough at that moment and whatever he was going through at that time with his health and his life generally, at the moment the man's heart melted. The barrier that he had put up seemed to fall away at this point. Following this, the man went to Confession and received Holy Communion. That prayer was a moment that brought about the change in this man's heart.

Opportunities to pray with people

We can all find ourselves in moments when there is an opportunity to pray for a person. Our prayer does not need to be long and theologically correct. We just pray from the heart and leave the rest to God. The more we do it, the easier it gets.

Here are some simple pointers about praying with a person.

First. We do need to choose the right moment. We should not force a situation. We need to be sensitive to the needs of the person. This is similar to what we have previously described as the red, yellow and green traffic lights. It is all about the right moment. Often this is determined by the other person.

Second. It is good to be as specific as possible in our prayer. This, of course, will depend on what the particular situation of the person is and what the person asks for. If the person has asked for a specific prayer, for example to be healed of a terminal disease, then ask for that in the prayer. The more specific the better.

Third. The prayer doesn't have to be long and complicated but rather simple and sincere. It is the moment and the grace and not the length of the prayer that matters. If the prayer is for healing then it should be directed to Jesus as he is the healer. If the person seeks to find God, then ask God to come to them and reveal Himself to them.

Fourth. If it is appropriate and if you feel comfortable lay your hand on the shoulder of the person. Human touch is very important as it creates a link with the person. Just like Jesus touched the leper.

We are truly missionary disciples if we are willing to be conduits of God's grace and mercy by praying for a person. Opportunities will present themselves. This is the moment which can be a decisive moment of grace for that person in their time of need.

Question for personal reflection

Am I ready to pray with a person when the opportunity arises?

15

We have a treasure

Pope Francis has presented us with a new and fresh way of seeing ourselves as Catholics: we are missionary disciples. When we accept this way of being Catholic then it has obvious implications for how we conduct our lives. In particular, as we have been considering, we need to orient ourselves outwards, towards the world. This is not only what the Church expects of us, but it is clearly what the Lord himself envisaged his followers would do. They were to be his witnesses "to the ends of the earth".

We considered in the previous chapter that this witness can lead us to being active agents for the grace of God to touch people's lives. When we pray with a person we are being the means by which God can act upon them. This is a privileged mission given to us.

As daunting as it may seem from the outset, it can become integral to the way in which we engage with people around us.

Our faith as a treasure

In St Matthew's Gospel, Chapter 13:44, we read the Lord saying,

> The kingdom of heaven is like treasure hidden in a field, which a man found and covered up; then in his joy he goes and sells all that he has and buys that field.

When a person encounters Christ, or has a profound spiritual experience, or truly discovers the reality of God, they realise that they have a received a treasure. In the parable, the man covers up the treasure so that he can arrange his life to be able to buy the field and have the treasure. In other words, he realises that this treasure is worth everything and everything else is of secondary importance.

We Catholics have a treasure: the treasure of our personal faith, of our living relationship with God, of our knowledge of Christ and his teaching. If we take a moment to consider what our faith means to us then we do realise what a treasure it is.

The treasure of the faith can be seen in many ways. We realise that our faith offers us a great sense of security about our life, about it's purpose and meaning, and destiny. It has provided, time and time again, consolation during dark times and difficulty.

We know that God loves me unconditionally and is always with me. We realise that God's love, like the sun, is always there, and I can always turn and draw on that love. I know that when I am burdened by my own sinfulness I can go to God and receive forgiveness and mercy. In these moments I receive a healing of my soul. I am set free and can move forward with new hope and purpose.

When we reflect upon living a life of faith, we realise what a great treasure we have. The more we appreciate it as a treasure, the more we realise that we should share this with others, especially with those people whose lives are in darkness, in a fog, in uncertainty. This gives us an incentive to want to offer to others what we know is a real treasure in our lives.

We are all aware that our society is changing. There has been a significant decline in religious affiliation. The number of those who claim to have no faith has risen dramatically. We are also aware that there is a growing antagonism towards Christianity. We can be tempted to withdraw and be silent. There is no doubt that Christianity is being subject to increasing attack. This is likely to increase in the time ahead.

However, as Christianity is marginalised in our society there will be a growing void in many people's lives. And many ordinary folk are searching and open to find purpose and meaning. While they may not identify this need as a need for God, this is, in fact, what is lacking in their lives.

Those who say that they are spiritual but not religious are saying that they still believe that there is a higher power, a supreme being and a spiritual dimension to life. This should be taken as a positive for us and an encouragement to help people find what they are searching for.

As believers, we can help bring this fullness of understanding to that which is the missing dimension in a person's life. We should not allow the antagonism, criticism, negativity, attacks and persecution that we experience to become the determining factor in how we relate to other people. The bulk of people who don't have a faith now do have a need to discover God, even if they do not realise it.

We should not feel that we do not have something to offer. Let us not withdraw and live our life privately but instead try to reach out and engage other people. When we look at people around us that don't have faith, I believe it is helpful to presume that they are searching. Thus, we wait for an opportunity which may come when we can witness to our faith.

Open wide to Christ

At his first Mass as newly elected Pope, Pope Benedict, in April 2005, said these words at the end of his homily.

> If we let Christ into our lives, we lose nothing, nothing, absolutely nothing of what makes life free, beautiful, and great. No! Only in this friendship are the doors of life opened wide... Yes, open, open wide the doors to Christ and you will find true life.

Pope Benedict reminds us of the truth that a person coming

to Christ will not experience a constriction of their life but rather be released into the fullness of life. Christianity truly sets a person free, and opens up vistas whereby they discover the beauty of human life. Faith in Christ enables a person to blossom and flourish fully in this life. And it opens up life to eternal union with God.

Salvation is but a breath away

I was recently approached by the family of a lady who had had a stroke and had slipped into a coma. The doctors were not hopeful and had told the family that this was possibly the end. The lady was not a Catholic and had no particular faith, but her husband was Catholic with a strong faith. Through her husband she had been exposed to the Catholic faith.

Surprisingly, the lady came out of her coma, and she said that during the coma she experienced a priest coming to her telling her to wake up. However, there had been no priest that had come to visit her during this time. She asked to see me as I had come to know the family. I then came to visit her in hospital. She asked for a blessing which I gave.

I was struck by the fact that even though she was not Catholic, there was a deep need in her for God. She had received some grace while in a coma.

We should never underestimate what may be in people's hearts, the desires people have in them, or what may be moments of grace whereby something touches them and they reach out for God.

Become Missionary Disciples

Let us become missionary disciples! Let us live as missionary disciples. Let us allow ourselves be to instruments of God's ongoing work of bringing people under the grace of salvation.

When the opportunity comes to share our faith let us be ready.

Question for personal reflection

Am I ready to become a missionary disciple?

About the author

Archbishop Julian Porteous was ordained a priest for the Archdiocese of Sydney in 1974. He has had extensive experience in parish ministry as well as involvement in renewal movements in the Church. Over the nearly 50 years of his priestly ministry he has been committed to promoting the need for evangelisation to be at the heart of the mission of the Church. He was appointed Rector of the Seminary of Good Shepherd, Sydney, in 2000. In 2003 he became Auxiliary Bishop in Sydney and appointed by Pope Francis as Archbishop of Hobart in 2013. He is the author of a number of books on pastoral and spiritual subjects.

www.ingramcontent.com/pod-product-compliance
Lightning Source LLC
Chambersburg PA
CBHW070555160426
43199CB00014B/2513